W9-CIO-494

How to Make Cowboy Horse Gear

Bruce Grant

**With a
section on
"How to Make
a Western Saddle"
by
Lee M. Rice**

CORNELL
MARITIME PRESS
Centreville, Maryland

Copyright © 1953, 1956 by Cornell Maritime Press, Inc.
Renewed 1981, 1984 by Catherine B. Grant

All rights reserved. No part of this book may be reproduced in any
manner whatsoever without written permission except in the case of
brief quotations embodied in critical articles and reviews. For information, address Cornell Maritime Press, Inc., Centreville, Maryland 21617.

ISBN 0-87033-034-9

Library of Congress Catalog Card Number: 56-10884

Manufactured in the United States of America
First edition, 1953. Second edition, 1956. 1990 reprint

LET US EXPLAIN AND ACKNOWLEDGE

Since my book, *Leather Braiding,* appeared in the spring of 1950 there have been many requests for more detailed instructions on how to make practical and decorative braided articles—especially horse gear. *Leather Braiding* was the first attempt to provide general knowledge on the subject of rawhide and leather braiding—the first book of its kind published in the English language.

Leather Braiding, for the most part, is concerned with showing the various types of braids and the step-by-step manner of making them. In this book are to be found the necessary braids for making all types of cowboy gear—*reatas* (rawhide lariats), headstalls, hackamores, bosals, reins, romals, quirts, hobbles, etc., as well as the general types of utility articles, such as dog leashes and collars, belts, hatbands, wrist-watch straps, etc.

To meet the demand for more specific detail, *How to Make Cowboy Horse Gear* was published in 1953. Its popularity was gratifying and the first edition was soon exhausted. A new and enlarged edition is now offered. Details for making any article of horse gear are given, with the types of braids to be used and how they are made, with the final steps and assembly of each piece of gear.

For those who wish to vary or elaborate on their braiding techniques, and make certain articles after their own fashion, they may employ the specifications for such articles as given in this book and choose types of braiding sequences found in the book *Leather Braiding.*

I thank the following for the loan of various braided articles, pictures, and for information and encouragement: Frank Barber, Red Bluff, California; Jim Breslin, La Junta, Colorado; John Conrad, Bellflower, California; Dan Delaney, Daniel, Wyoming; Tom Dorrance, Joseph, Oregon; J. E. Draper, publisher of *Horse Lover* magazine; Mrs. Mary Fields, Bonanza, Oregon; L. H. Hamley of Hamley & Company, Pendleton, Oregon; Roy Harmon, Las Cruces, New Mexico; Wright Howes, Chicago; Ernie Ladouceur,

Madera, California; Douglas Lamoreaux, Winton, California; Lee M. Rice, San Leandro, California; Edward R. Rickman, Fishtail, Montana; Burt Rogers, Spearfish, South Dakota; L. H. Rutter, Hinsdale, Montana; Duff Severe, Pendleton, Oregon; Jim Shaw, Lander, Wyoming; Dick Spencer III, editor, *Western Horseman* magazine; Randy Steffen, *Western Horseman* magazine; Edward Larocque Tinker, New York City; Karl Vogel, New York City; Jesse Wilkinson, Paso Robles, California.

And a special word of thanks to: George Kotalik, TIMES Photographer, Chicago, Illinois, for additional photographs in this new edition; the *Western Horseman* for permission to reprint the diagram and text of "That Ole Fiador Knot," and Mario Pagliai, Highwood, Illinois, for his artistic efforts on the original plates in the first edition.

Bruce Grant

CONTENTS

THE ROMANCE OF RAWHIDE

Rawhide is a tradition —not merely a word. It is the story of the Old West from the brushhopper to the cowpuncher, from cow-hunts to roundups, from the open plains to fenced-in ranches, from the chaparral country clear up that course of an empire, the Texas Trail. The story is tied together in tough and lasting rawhide.

Rawhide has been called both "Indian Iron" and "Mexican Iron." As the Indian *shaganappi,* the Mormons employed it to lash together the beams of their temple at Salt Lake City. As *cuero crudo,* the Southwestern cowboys used it for making quirts, head-stalls, *reatas,* bosals, and reins, and softened it into *latigos,* or saddle tie-strings and belts. Nothing has been found better suited to cover a saddle tree.

The Apaches shod their horses with rawhide shoes. When an iron band broke on the wheel of an old-time prairie schooner, it might be replaced with a rawhide rim. The fur-trappers, or "moun-tain men," made moccasins from the smoke-impregnated, and thus unshrinkable, rawhide coverings of their winter lodges. Indians converted deerskin rawhide into the softest buckskin.

They say Texas was bound together with rawhide. Texans were known to northern cowboys as "rawhides," because of their custom of repairing anything with the material,—from bridles to wagon tongues. A "rawhide" was an affectionate name for an old-timer. "Rawhiding" in cowboy lingo meant to torture or abuse, or to verbally "ride." It also meant to *thrash.* Rawhide lumber was cottonwood slabs. There were even "rawhide" ponies.

We could go on to tell how green rawhide strings with their marvelous power of constriction, were used to lash together corral posts; how rawhide was employed in making all types of ranch fur-niture; how the "jewel box" of the chuck-wagon contained an as-sortment of rawhide strings and pieces for repairs; or how slung beneath the wagon itself was the "cooney", a rawhide apron for carrying fuel,—usually buffalo or cow chips. But our main object is to tell about *rawhide-making* and *rawhide-braiding.*

Literature on the subject is scarce. One might say that it does not exist, for the few and scattered items on rawhide-making are superficial and take too much for granted. As to rawhide braiding, there is nowhere to be found a comprehensive treatise on the subject.

As to rawhide-making, one might conjecture that the apparent basic simplicity of the process needs no explanation. Rawhide just makes itself. A cowboy or Indian skinned his animal, stretched the hide and then scraped off the hair. There was little else to it.

Therein lies the delusion. It is much like learning Spanish; it seems so easy at first, then opens up a life-long study. Or like an Air Corps officer said about flying: "A novice can solo after a few hours in the air, but it takes him five years to learn to fly."

In preparing this book I have gone, as it were, right to the feed-bag. I have corresponded with men who make and work their own rawhide, who are scattered throughout the West and Southwest and up into Canada. Such men deserve much of the credit for preserving and making known the possibilities of this traditional handicraft.

It is heartening to know that there still are some fine rawhide makers and braiders who carry on their work with rawhide that amounts to a reverential regard for their material. One man I know seeks out these old-timers to sit at their knee, like the youth of Athens in the presence of Socrates. And I will never forget, as he once wrote me, that he had found Pinkie Bethel up in the Sierras—a fellow who had been working rawhide for fifty years—and came upon him when he was actually at work braiding.

"I suddenly realized," wrote my friend, Ernie Ladouceur, of Madera, California, "that I had never before seen one of these old-timers actually braiding rawhide. I had seen much of his stuff and much of the fancy work of others, but this was the first time I had seen one of these men at work."

John Conrad, of Bellflower, California, is an expert professional braider, and has this to say:

"To most people the word 'Rawhide' carries little significance; but to many old-timers, like myself, it brings back fond memories of an episode in life that will never be forgotten.

"Back in the late Nineties, I was a member of a family who pioneered far from the railhead, out on the Canadian prairies. By our own resourcefulness and assistance of friendly Indians, we managed to overcome most of our difficulties, and I remember, with much gratitude, the Indian brave who taught me my first lessons in bronco-busting and cow-punching.

"Living several hundred miles from a small town, which had no saddle shops, I early learned the virtues of rawhide, which I was able to produce in a crude manner. We used it for riding equipment, to string up our bunks, and make the bedrolls more comfortable; also for chair seats and backs, and to lash together rails and posts, because we had no nails.

"From the beginning, I have always had a sentimental regard for rawhide, which I feel played as big a part in our pioneer existence as gunpowder. In later years my hobby has been the designing and making of rawhide articles, still very usable, but considerably more artistic, than those we made fifty years ago."

Many, many stories could be told of the part rawhide played in winning the West.

Rawhide and leather braiding are among the oldest of crafts. They could well be the oldest, as prehistoric man had to use hide and skin thongs to join things together and so may early have discovered the virtues of the *braided rope.*

Braiding is uniquely a creation of man and developed from the necessity for a strong and satisfactory fastening, first by simple thonging, and later from the creature's desire to make this utility measure a thing of beauty.

Braidwork is not merely show. Generally, the craft serves some practical purpose to which its decorative effect is a pleasing addition. A leather or rawhide strap cut into four thongs or strings and braided is stronger than the original strap itself.

When we say braiding is a creation of man, we mean just that. There is no braidwork in nature. Despite the beautiful and symmetric patterns found in nature's work, her minutely intricate yet systematic way of "knitting" things together, nowhere is there to be found what can be classified as an actual braid, a plait or a weave.

The spider's web is not woven but laid together, gossamer strand upon gossamer strand, held together by a sort of cement. The cocoon is not a braid but a wrapping, and the skeletal pattern of a leaf, while having the appearance of a weave or braid, is only a simulation of the latter. Vines and such which interweave themselves in forests do not follow any rule—it is only by chance we find them braided together.

The early Egyptians had a knowledge of braiding or weaving, as seen in the cloth enshrouding their mummies. The presence of leather in Egyptian tombs also indicates that these people were expert tanners and, after more than a thousand years, the leather has been found to be in fair condition.

However, the earliest period which historians can fix for leather tanning and the use of leather in craftsmanship is during the days of the Phœnicians. There is a story of how Queen Dido, about 822 B.C., in acquiring a piece of land upon which to erect the city of Carthage in North Africa, was told by the native chief, Iarbas, she could have "as much land as could be contained in the skin of an ox." The wise queen had the ox hide cut in a long thin thong around and around the edge in spiral fashion and this thong enclosed an entire hill upon which Queen Dido built a fort.

The rawhide worker in cutting his strings uses this method today. He cuts them in spiral fashion from a "round" of hide or skin.

The Phœnicians imparted their knowledge to the Arabs and these people of the desert used it to good advantage in making their saddles, bridles, whips,—in fact, everything that applied to the horse. It is from that time on that fancy rawhide and leather braiding—with leather carving and saddle decoration—was to be associated with this noble creature, the horse.

When the Moors overran Spain they took with them their leather craftsmen. It was in Spain that the art of leatherwork, particularly braiding, was to reach its highest development.

Hernando Cortes brought with him the leather artists to Mexico and Don Pedro de Mendoza introduced the craft into South America during the early part of the sixteenth century. Thus we find a definite kinship between the work of the Argentine *gaucho* and the Mexican *vaquero*. It had a common source.

In this book I have included three pictures which illustrate this. One is that of an old Arabian knife, another of a South American quirt or *rebenque,* and the third of a Mexican quirt. On each will be found the same woven knot, thus showing how with the art of braiding, this knot passed along from Arabia to Spain, thence to North and South America.

The Mexican *vaquero,* who was also a *trenzador,* or braider, kept his art flourishing in old California and in *Tejas,* or Texas.

Still later, too, when he hit the trail with his cattle herds from below the Border, he brought along his knowledge of braidwork and inspired our own cowboys in the craft of making fancy gear.

There are still some who can remember this time, among them Jim Breslin, of La Junta, Colorado. In a letter to the author, he states:

"All the Mexican cowpunchers that came up with trail herds in the '80's and early '90's tied these Spanish knots, and did beautiful rawhide work. And today it is almost a lost art."

Knowledge of rawhide braiding also was brought directly to the United States by the intrepid and picturesque Basque. Many of them settled in the far West. I located a rawhide braider, unfortunately in a western prison at the time, who wrote me that "the basic elements of rawhide braiding were gathered by me from Mexican and Basque leather artists."

This particular man was one of those who did not wish to reveal the secrets of his craft. He was confident that none could duplicate his work, and made this offer:

"I have never seen any of my work duplicated and . . . if you purchase any of my items and can produce an exact duplicate within 60 days, I will refund double your money along with the duplicate."

These articles consisted of an 8-string square-braided steerhide pair of reins and romal at $20; matching quirt at $7.50 and a 6-string round-braided pair of rawhide reins (10 foot type) at $7.50. The craftsman felt secure in this offer, and for the main part I would say rightly so. His confidence lay in his knowledge of one or possibly two braided knots.

Usually so-called braiding "secrets" were handed down from father to son. As braiding was supplanted by commercial articles fastened together with metal brads, buckles, and other attachments, and decorated with outlandish "horse jewelry", the art began to decline.

Then, too, from the American viewpoint, it took too much time. There is no craftsman today, who, while exhibiting a piece of beautiful handiwork, is not familiar with the first disconcerting question, "How long did it take you?" That is all important. The number of hours it takes to complete something and the price a man charges for each hour of work.

I have only one answer for such a question. It is that "it has taken me thirty years to make this article." It may have taken but a few hours, but one must consider the actual period of time consumed in reaching the perfection stage.

If braiding could be done by machinery, on a production line basis, it would be acceptable. But as a profession or occupation whereby one makes a living, it is outmoded. So the son rarely cares to learn from the father and take up braiding as a profession or calling.

From our viewpoint this is fortunate. It means the old-timers for the most part no longer care to protect their "secrets". We can learn more from them and so spread the knowledge. Braiding can become an occupation for anyone who wants to make his own horse-gear or the many other beautiful and practical articles to which it lends itself.

Then, too, people are becoming more conscious of the old West and its customs and craft lore. With dude ranching, western movies on the screen and television, and the desire of the more noble-minded folk to breed and foster the horses of bye-gone days, there has come once more the desire to caparison the princely brute in all the decorative trappings to which he is rightly entitled.

There is nothing as dressy and serviceable in horse gear as braid-work,—rawhide braidwork, especially. It is richer looking and stronger than gear made from plain strap leather. It is far more decorative, and more in order, than a lot of ornate and heavy "horse jewelry".

In braidwork you can dispense with all buckles, brads, and other metal fastenings. A headstall can be made adjustable by a series of braided knots and buttons. This is one of the primary objects of such work, to hold pieces of leather and rawhide together as in ancient days when no metal fastenings existed.

There are old-timers who remember the days when braided headstalls, reins, breast-collars, and other horse-gear were common-place equipment,—so familiar to those good fellows that they never bothered to learn how they were made, or how the braiding was done. Now that this type of work has begun to disappear, they regret having missed the opportunity of learning the craft.

People write me in this vein: "I used to know a fellow who would come around to the ranch and do this work. Now I'm sorry I didn't pay more attention to him." True, these braiders often were a bit cagey in letting others see how the work was done.

Some, however, would have been glad to share their knowledge with the interested inquirer.

I recall one fellow who wrote me that the only opportunity he ever had to learn braidwork was from a left-handed braider. He would watch and study the craftsman's methods, but somehow could never get the hang of the thing—he could not transfer the technique to his own right-handed way of working. In the end he was just plumb confused and gave up!

Horsemen should strive today to keep alive the tradition of rawhide and rawhide braiding—and leather braiding, too—that remarkable contribution to the horsemanship of the West and Southwest.

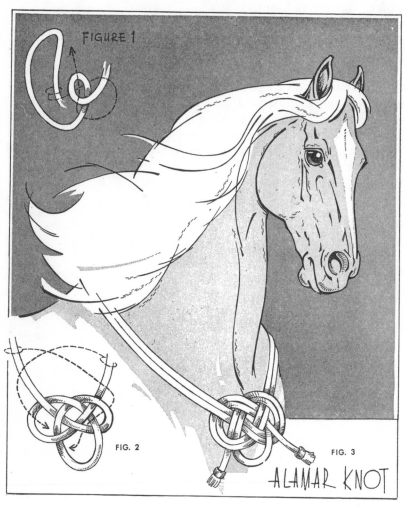

FIGURE 1

FIG. 2

FIG. 3

ALAMAR KNOT

Alamar, a Spanish word meaning *gimp,* or decoration, is a name given to this knot or weave by the Spanish Caballero who used it to "dike" out his Caballo for parades and state functions.

PLATE 1

MAKING AND WORKING RAWHIDE

Some readers of this book will be in a position to make their own rawhide. Others will have to buy it.

Those who wish to work with leather most likely will have to go to a leather dealer or handicraft store to obtain their leather or cut thongs and lacing.

First let us talk about *boughten* rawhide. The kinds of rawhide that can be easily purchased include those used for making drumheads, artificial limbs, and other commercial articles. This prepared hide can be used by the braider, who soaks it in water and cuts it into strings. There is also a product termed "rawhide" which is oil-packed and more pliable. But shy away from a commercial product called "rawhide" that is a greasy, sleazy stuff used for shoe laces. It is no good for braiding.

As to leather, most handicraft or hobby shops carry a commercial type of leather lacing or thonging. This lacing comes in several widths, but the 1/8- and 3/32-inch widths are the most popular. It also is to be had in a variety of colors. *Goat skin* lacing is stronger and more durable; *calf skin* is more dressy. Such lacing can be used in braiding. Various types of plastic or composition lacing also may be found in such shops, and I have seen some fancy headstalls and reins made from that material.

Leather, too, can be purchased in skins, hides, or kips. *Skins* are from the smaller animals like the calf, goat, deer, etc., and *hides* are from the cow, steer, horse, moose, and larger animals. *Kips* are from mature, but smaller or undersized animals. From all these, satisfactory thongs may be cut.

Leather-making, or tanning, is a long and difficult process; so it is best to buy your leather. But anyone with a back yard or small out-door space can make good *rawhide*. (Douglas Lamoreaux of Winton, Cal., shows how on pages 12 & 13.) Nature does most of the work. It is best to obtain the hide or skin as soon as possible after the animal has been killed, and before it is dried out. This is known as a "green hide". If it has been dried out without being salted or treated with chemicals, it is known as a "flint hide". Flint hides can be used if they have not been dried in the sun, but "salt hides", or those treated chemically, are not good for rawhide strings, except under certain circumstances which will later be referred to. Such hides have lost some of their "life".

In working with the green hide, first stake it out on the ground or other place in the shade for about two hours. Nothing more has to be done, for it will change of its own accord from the green hide to rawhide. In *Fig. 1, Plate 1,* is shown the proper way to stake out a hide, pulling it in the direction of the arrows so it will "set" as near round as possible.

After it has been staked for two hours it is stiff enough to work with. Trim off the hanging bits of flesh on the flesh side of the hide and cut it into a round or oval shape (*Fig. 1*). That is, find the center of the hide and make a large circle, or oblong, which will eliminate the legs, neck, and other outside parts.

Cut this disk, or oblong piece, into a strip about 2 or 2½ inches wide by going round and round the circle until you get to the center. This can be done with heavy shears or a sharp knife (*Fig. 2*). In the thinner portions of the hide, such as the belly, cut the strip slightly wider. When the strip dries it will shrink to about two-thirds of its width.

Be attentive to what is known as the moisture control, that is, if the strip becomes too dry to cut easily, dampen the hide. Then fasten one end of this long strip to a post and, holding it taut with the left hand, shave off the hair with a sharp knife. Do not cut the top or scarf skin as this is the tough part and in it lies the strength of your string.

There are other ways to dehair rawhide. If it is calf skin or deer skin, the hair will usually slip if the skin has been soaked four or five days in running water. But the hair on cowhides and steerhides comes away less easily. These can be soaked in a "milk" of lime and water. Take one part quick lime and fifteen parts water. When the lime has been slaked place the strip in it for four or five days. The hair should then come off easily.

Douglas Lamoreaux, of Winton, California, suggests that after removing the hair with lime—either slaked or dehydrated lime— wash it in several baths of cool running water and then soak it for twenty-four hours in thirty gallons of water containing three ounces of lactic acid. This will neutralize the lime and make a more pliable rawhide.

In removing the hair, the back of a butcher knife, or an old file

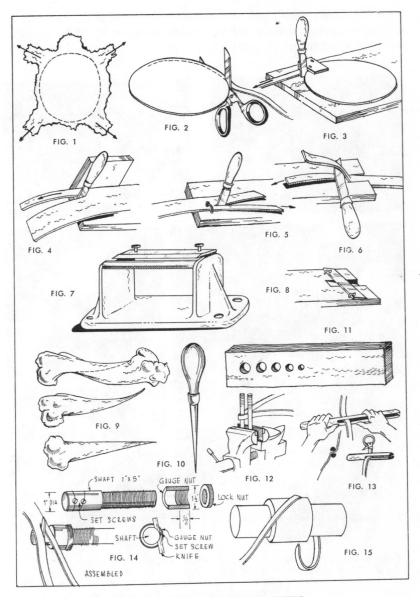

FIG. 1

FIG. 2

FIG. 3

FIG. 4

FIG. 5

FIG. 6

FIG. 7

FIG. 8

FIG. 11

FIG. 9

FIG. 10

FIG. 12

FIG. 13

SHAFT 1"X 5"   GAUGE NUT
1" DIA   LOCK NUT
SET SCREWS
SHAFT   GAUGE NUT
                              SET SCREW
FIG. 14   KNIFE
ASSEMBLED

FIG. 15

PLATE 1. MAKING AND WORKING RAWHIDE

with the edges smoothed and slightly rounded, are good implements to employ. Stick the point of the butcher knife in a round piece of wood to give a good hand "holt" on that end. In the case

Steps in making rawhide. *A.* Hide spread on ground. *B.* Washing and soaking. Hide soaked in lime or hardwood ash solution to loosen hair. *C.* Putting hide over dehairing post, hair side out. *D.* Pushing or slipping off the hair. *E.* Placing hide in drying frame. *F.* Removing excess flesh and fat from flesh side. *G.* Buffing flesh side. This is done after hide has dried out and can be done by hand. *H.* After cutting hide out of drying frame. *I.* Long strip of hide made by cutting around the hide in spiral fashion, stretched between posts and allowed to dry for several days. This strip is about 2 inches wide. *J.* Cutting strings from long strip. Here machinery is used. But this can be done by hand.

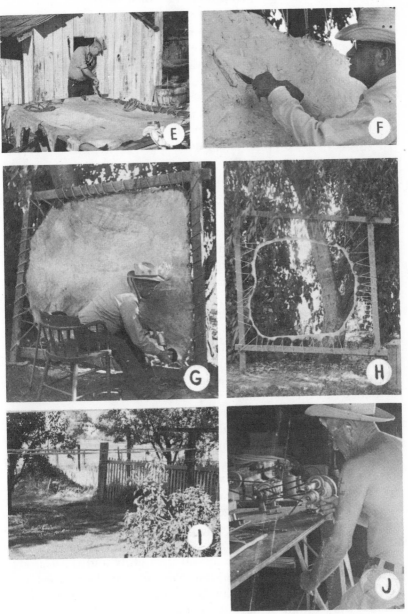

Steps in making rawhide.

of the file, it can be sunk into a groove in a round piece of wood, with about ¼ inch of the edge protruding.

A mixture of wood ashes and water is a good dehairer. The best ashes come from hardwood. Make this into a soupy paste in a tub and soak the hide in it for forty-eight hours. In a pinch you can wet the hide and sprinkle the ashes on the hair side and roll it up. Wrap a damp burlap cloth around it and leave it for a few days. Slip the hair without removing the ashes.

Jim Shaw, of Lander, Wyoming, ran across an old taxidermy book which detailed a couple of ways of removing hair from a hide. Jim has passed this information along:

"The usual method of loosening the hair is by the use of lime and red arsenic. These are made into a thick paste and slaked together, by adding a small amount of water. After slaking, more water is added and the mixture is smeared on the hair side of the hide. The hide is now folded together, hair side in. The hair slips in one or more days."

Red arsenic (arsenic disulphide) can be replaced by sodium sulphide and used in the same way. The formula for this would be: one gallon of boiling water; ½ cake of brown soap, shaved; cool and add one heaping tablespoon of sodium sulphide and one pint of dry unslacked lime, the last two to be slaked together and then added to the solution.

Jim Shaw suggests scraping off the bulk of the hair as soon as it starts to slip, then putting the hide back into the solution with a handful of borax, which cleans the hide. As a neutralizing agent, he favors one quart of chicken manure to a gallon of water, or boracic (boric) acid or lactic acid.

"Another method that is easiest of all, as no solutions are involved," continues Jim, "I learned from an old rawhider in Washington. The only stickler is you have to get the hide with the body heat still in it. If you can do this, fold the hide from each side with the hair on the inside and roll up tightly and tie securely. In a day or two the hair slips and the hide can be scraped and stretched. However, if you have to, you can leave the hair on for several days without damage if the hide is unrolled every day for an hour or so of airing. This makes good, firm rawhide and it seems to have more life and body than ordinary rawhide. I have an old bosal that was made of an eight-braid without core, yet it has more life than most cored commercial bosals."

After the hair has been taken off, the long strip of rawhide should be stretched between two trees or posts—in the shade—and allowed to dry thoroughly. Leave it strung up for four or five days. When it is dry it is ready to be cut into strings.

If flint hides are used they should be "tempered". After being soaked until there are no hard spots you can rub in saddle soap, using it as it comes from the can, or plain yellow laundry soap. Neatsfoot oil or tallow, if used, make the hide water proof and hard to dampen for reworking.

Simple as rawhide-making is, there is always something to learn about it. Recently I was told of an old Texas method of making it and I have found it very good. This is a "salt method", but produces a different skin than the *salt-cured* hide, which is not suitable for rawhide braiding. For instructions on the procedure involved I am indebted to Ed Rickman, who says he learned it from an old Texan named Sonny Strong. Sonny Strong has passed over the Great Divide, but his way of making rawhide lives on.

This is it: When the hide or skin is taken off the carcass and while the body heat is still in it, spread it out flat with the flesh side up and salt it down with 40 or 50 pounds of fine stock salt. This is for a mature hide. For a yearling or calf skin use half the amount of salt. Spread the salt evenly and fold the hide over so the hair side is out and the flesh sides are together.

Leave the hide in a shady, dry place for from a week to ten days. It is important to salt the hide while the body heat is still in it, Rickman emphasizes. So if you do not actually remove the hide yourself, get the person who does the work to salt it down for you. The salt runs the blood and glue out of the hide before it congeals and Rickman feels this is important in keeping the hide pliable.

When the hide has reached the consistency of stiff bread dough after a week or so, spread it out and split it down the back into two parts. Next cut into strips lengthwise. These strips should be about three inches wide. Lay a gunny sack on your knee, take a strip of the hide and, with a sharp knife—we mean sharp!—grain off the hair. Pull the strip toward you as you cut with the knife blade almost flat. Instead of scraping the hair you will be splitting it off at the roots. This takes off the top grain of the hide, and it should be cut off smoothly. Turn the strip over and flesh it down to good solid hide. These fine tissues on the flesh side make the hide hard when dry. Get them off.

Now you can roll the strip up and let it dry for future use, or you can cut it into strings right away. If you are going to let it dry and cut it later you will have to soak it in a can of *salt* water until it is soft,—not soggy, but pliable like leather.

Rickman, instead of splitting his strip, rubs down the flesh side by pulling it back and forth over a shoeing rasp. Place the rasp in a vise and pull the strip of rawhide back and forth across it. This evens the hide throughout its length and no splitting is necessary. However, do not rub the hair side against the rasp—the flesh side only.

This is an entirely different way of making rawhide, and may be considered by many old-timers as unorthodox. I have worked with such rawhide and it is very strong and more pliable than the ordinary kind.

If you wish to use the *Indian method,* then merely let the hide dry out, after being staked to the ground. Indians sometimes dry it in the sun. Soak it two days in running water, remove it, scrape off the hair and flesh, and it is ready for use. Indians save this hair and flesh for making a kind of soup; but I presume we can skip that. The hide is softened by rubbing in the cooked brains and liver. It is made waterproof by smoking it. This is *buckskin.*

If you want to do very fine work with narrow strings, the rawhide strip should first be split to a uniform thickness. In such a case it is run through a splitter. Previous to this it must be soaked in water until no hard spots are felt, and then wrapped in a damp cloth and allowed to mellow for an hour or so. There is a point where rawhide is neither too damp nor too dry and cuts perfectly.

The best type of splitter is that used by harness-makers *(Fig. 7).* This consists of two uprights about six inches in height and ten inches apart, bolted to a heavy metal base. A thick-backed, thin-edged knife is fastened to the uprights in such a way that it is adjustable and movable to and from a machined steel roller, which is below it and parallel to it. By adjusting the knife the rawhide can be split any thickness desired. This method is used also for leather thongs, of course.

For a home-made splitter I am indebted to Dan Delaney, an old-time cowboy who works with the Hoodoo Outfit in Daniel, Wyoming. This is shown in *Figs. 6* and *8.* Cut a notch on the edge of a board—notch slanting down into the edge. Over this notch fasten a knife (Delaney nails on a mower section). Start the strip of rawhide through the notch, flesh side up. By moving the knife forward or backward the thickness may be increased or decreased. An ordinary knife can be held over the notch by pressure of the hand.

With the strip (or "soga", as it was known in the old days along the Border) of a uniform thickness, you now cut it into *strings*. (It will be noted that the term "strings" is used for rawhide and "thongs" for leather.)

There are several ways of cutting strings. Bill Phillips, of Savona, British Columbia, takes a board of soft wood and nails it to a bench or the floor. Then he drives a No. 7 horseshoe nail *(Fig. 5)* solidly into the center of the board, with the flat of the nail along the grain. The nail is bent over sharply so that the bent part lies parallel to the board's surface, with enough space between nail and board to accommodate the rawhide. Point of the knife is pushed into the wood with the keen edge against the nail, at a distance from the upright part of the nail equal to desired width of the string. The blade may be set at an angle to bevel the strings as they are cut. This bevel would thus run on the hair side of one edge of the string and on the flesh side of the other. The knife may be moved to make wider or narrower strings.

Also is shown a cutter designed by Doug Lamoreaux which may be clamped in a vise *(Fig. 14)*. It has two slits *(A* and *B)* for placing the blade to cut a beveled edge or a vertical edge. Doug estimates that this gadget can be made for approximately five dollars.

As to beveling rawhide strings and leather thongs, the rawhide usually is beveled on the hair side and the leather on the flesh side. The reason for beveling the rawhide on the hair side is that otherwise the sharp edges curl upward in drying. Beveling prevents this and gives a smooth finish to the braid. A thick thong of leather beveled on the flesh side allows it to lie snug. In some wide thongs, the bevel is on the hair side on one edge and the flesh side on the other. These edges overlap on the alternate thongs.

In *Fig. 3* is shown a cutter where the string or thong is made from a small round or disc of leather or rawhide. In such a case, a 1/8" thong or string a yard long can be cut from a disc two inches in diameter; a three-inch disc yields two yards, and a four-inch disc three and one-half yards, and so on. In *Fig. 4* is another type of home-made cutter for cutting thongs or strings from long strips of leather or rawhide.

Old-time quirt and whip-makers sometimes use a sharp knife with the thumb as a guide in cutting strings and thongs freehand. In this manner they can taper the string or thong by moving the thumb toward the knife. This requires considerable practice.

If rawhide strings are to be softened they should be placed while damp in warm melted tallow or neatsfoot oil. They are then pulled back and forth against a round piece of wood held in a vise. Keep oiling them and working them around the wood as they dry out.

I have found a good way to soften strings, or even *sogas,* is to clamp two sections of a broom handle in a vise, about 1/4 inch apart *(Fig. 12).* Place the string or strip of rawhide around these as shown in the diagram and seesaw back and forth, keeping the string or strip well saddle-soaped. I am partial to saddle soap instead of tallow or neatsfoot oil, as I think the tallow and oil tend to deteriorate the rawhide, especially if it is left in the sun. Instead of saddle soap, good old yellow laundry soap may be used and is just as effective.

In the Argentine they have a good method of softening rawhide. Take a round piece of wood about 20 inches long (a broom handle is good) and two inches in diameter. Cut a slot through middle part of stick and round off the edges of the slot with a fine file. The string is fastened to a nail and its loose part is inserted in the slot of the "mordaza" or "sobador", as it is called. Turn the stick slightly so that it takes some effort to draw the string through the slot. Pull the softener for the entire length of the string and repeat until the string is soft like leather. Saddlesoap or oil is used during the softening.

In braiding rawhide it will sometimes be found that, when the finished braid dries, the strings have narrowed and daylight can be seen through them. This means they have been improperly tempered or have been worked while too wet. Rawhide workers dampen their strings until they are about like 12-minute spaghetti. They rub soap in them. If the string has little of the natural oil left in it the rawhider retempers it. To retemper strings, rub them well with saddle soap (or tallow or neatsfoot oil) and wrap them while damp in a piece of damp burlap and allow them to remain for forty-eight hours. If you use soap you can redampen these strings, while if you temper them with neatsfoot oil or tallow, once they dry out it is difficult to restore them to that pliable condition required for good work. So don't spare the soap.

You won't need many tools for braiding. A good, sharp knife is essential. Most important is a fid, or an instrument which tapers to a thin, rounded point,—*not a sharp one. (Fig. 10)*.

Fids can be made from bone. In fact, several of your tools may be made from bone,—soup bones, or those from the Sunday roast. With a hacksaw and file you can shape a piece of bone nicely. Polish it with steel wool and then some fine abrasive, such as pumice or rotten stone.

I turned out a very fine fid from the leg bone of a sheep. (Cattle men, please forget your prejudices for a moment). This bone had a slight curve to it and I took advantage of this curve in fashioning my fid. This is shown in the accompanying illustration, *(Fig. 9)*.

Another practical gadget can be made from a piece of thick bone, or hardwood. This is a gauge for round braid *(Fig. 11)*. A half dozen holes are drilled through the bone or wood with machine drills—say, starting with a 5/8, graduating down to a 1/16-inch hole. Bevel or smooth edges of the holes on both sides.

A round braid after being rolled under foot, is first drawn through the hole which is closest to its diameter. Then it is drawn through the next smaller hole; then the next smaller one. This evens up the braid and polishes it, and makes it of a consistent diameter throughout.

Several mandrels of various diameters are handy gadgets. They are used in making *turk's heads* and *braided knots*. One is shown in *Fig. 15*. This is a piece of broom handle with a leather or rawhide collar. The collar is to keep the knot from slipping while being braided. A face may be cut or filed on each of the four sides and these faces numbered in a clockwise direction from 1 to 4. This will help in the instructions which follow on braided knots.

THE ANATOMY OF THE TURK'S HEAD

Now let us be practical. The simplest form of braiding is the flat braid, or the so-called *hair-braid* of three thongs. This is working each outer thong alternately over the one nearest it toward the center.

Such a working procedure is the basis of flat braiding. Work your outer thongs in rotation—that is, each time bringing the highest thong on each side toward the center. If it passes over one thong and under one thong on one side, the thong on the other side also passes over one and under one.

But the hair-braid is not as simple as that. It may be made to form the toughest of all knots, the *turk's head,* which is nothing more than a flat braid made into a wreath or ring by means of a single thong.

The turk's head is a practical knot and an old sailor's favorite. But the braider should think of it as a foundation upon which to fashion the *woven-knot,* or the *Spanish Knot.* While it is customary for present-day braiders to double or triple the leather or rawhide turk's head by following around to make it larger or longer, this is a sailor's trick and is not practicable in leather or rawhide work. Why? Because leather thongs or rawhide strings will invariably overlap on the scallops; the round rope will not do this. The turk's head then should be used without being doubled or tripled, and only as a foundation knot, or at times by itself.

Now to simplify the turk's head let us look at its anatomy. It is usually tied in a different fashion from that explained in this chapter, but for those who are mystified by it, we are going to explain the easy way of making it.

Take three thongs and pin them down on a cardboard mailing-tube, or a round stick of wood, as shown in *Fig. 1, Plate 2.* The thongs are then worked into a three-part flat braid, or hair braid.

Thong A on the left is passed to the right over the middle thong B *(Fig. 1).* Thong C on the right is passed to the left over thong A *(Fig. 2).* In *Fig. 3* we pass thong B to the right over thong C. Observe *Fig. 4* carefully. The braid has been continued by alternately passing the thong on each side over the one next to it and to the center. We have formed a braid which has three "bights", "loops", or "scallops" on the edges *(Fig. 4)*.

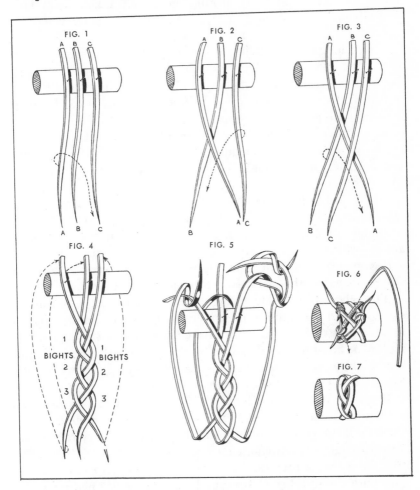

PLATE 2. THE ANATOMY OF THE TURK'S HEAD

The working or business end of thong A is now on the lower right hand side; that of thong C in the middle, and that of thong B on the lower left hand side. These three ends should be passed back under the tube (or round stick) in the same relationship and joined with the standing ends of those at the top. The working end of thong B is tied to the standing end of thong A; the working end of thong C to B, and the working end of A to C *(Fig. 5)*.

In *Fig. 6* the ends are shown joined together. Pick any part of a thong and start following around with your finger, over knots and all, and you will find that you return to the place where you started. Thus you have formed a *turk's head*.

Take a long thong and, just as you passed your finger around, pass the thong around until the working end comes back and joins the standing end, or starting point. Then untie the original thongs and pull them clear and you will find that your long thong has formed a *three-part, four-bight turk's head (Fig. 7)*.

Remember we braided the flat braid down until it had three bights or scallops on each side *(Fig. 4)*. But, when the ends were tied together, another bight was formed on each side—making four bights on a side.

There is a rule to be observed in making turk's heads. A relationship exists between the bights, or scallops, and the number of thongs directly across the turk's head. By the number of thongs across—which we call "parts"—is meant that if you cut straight across the turk's head at right angles you would sever, in this case, three thongs. So this is called a *three-part turk's head*.

The relationship between bights and parts is this: The number of *bights* and the number of *parts* cannot have a common divisor. A three-part turk's head cannot have three bights, six bights, nine bights, or any number divisible by three. It can have two bights, four bights, five bights, seven bights, eight bights, or any number which cannot be divided by three.

If you try to tie a turk's head with bights and parts which have a common divisor, the ends will come together or meet before the knot is complete. Turk's heads are perfect in every respect and are the delight of mathematicians.

Always observe then the rule that no one number can be divided into both the number of parts and the number of bights of your turk's head.

The simple three-part flat braid and three-part turk's head do not constitute anything elaborate in braiding, but to know how to make them is important as a beginning. They illustrate how you can take any flat braid—one of four thongs, five thongs *(Figs. 1 and 2, Plate 3)*, six thongs, or any number up to infinity—and make from it a turk's head.

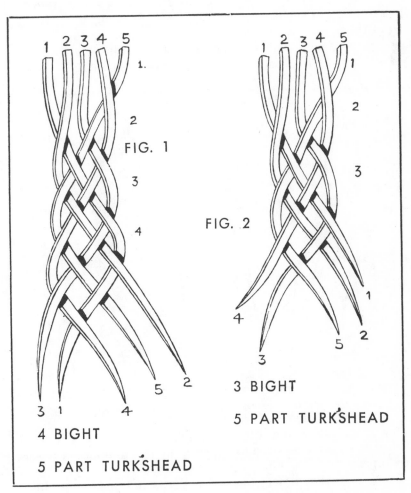

FIG. 1

FIG. 2

4 BIGHT
5 PART TURK'SHEAD

3 BIGHT
5 PART TURK'SHEAD

PLATE 3. THE ANATOMY OF THE TURK'S HEAD, *con't.*

Take a look at *Fig. 1, Plate 3.* Here is a *five-thong braid* which has been braided down until there are four bights on each side (including, of course, the bight which will be formed when the ends are tied together). To make this into a turk's head you tie the lower part of thong 3 to the upper part of thong 1; the lower part of thong 1 to the upper part of thong 2; lower 4 to upper 3; lower 5 to upper 4, and lower 2 to upper 5. Follow around and you will have a turk's head, of four bights and five parts.

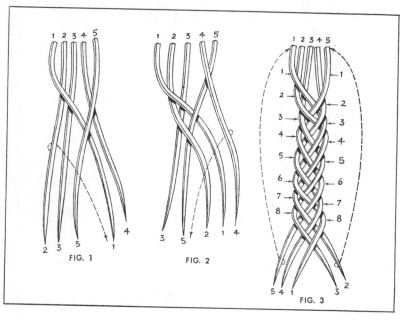

PLATE 4. THE ANATOMY OF THE TURK'S HEAD, *concluded*

In *Fig. 2, Plate 3,* is a three-bight, five-part turk's head. Lower 4 is tied to upper 1; lower 3 to upper 2; lower 5 to upper 3; lower 2 to upper 4, and lower 1 to upper 5.

There is another way to braid five thongs and make them into a turk's head. This is shown in *Figs. 1, 2* and *3* in *Plate 4.*

Take five thongs and first pass the one on the extreme left (thong 1) to the right and over two and to the center. Then take the thong on the extreme right, thong 5, and pass it to the left over two and to the center. Thong 2 on the left is next brought to the right over two. This is shown in *Fig. 1.*

In *Fig.* 2 we see thong 4 on the right has been passed to the center over two thongs. Then you work thong 3 toward the center and over two. Then thong 1 to the left, and so on.

In *Fig. 3* you will see the anatomy of the woven knot, which is commonly called the *Spanish Ring Knot*. We have braided down until there are eight bights or loops on each side (including the one which will be formed when the ends are joined). Now if you take the lower end of thong 5 and tie it to the upper end of thong 1; the lower end of thong 4 to the upper end of thong 2; the lower end of thong 1 to the upper end of thong 3; the lower end of thong 3 to the upper end of thong 4, and the lower end of thong 2 to the upper end of thong 5—then you will have the Spanish Ring Knot.

By starting at any point and passing your finger along over the joined thongs you will finally come back to the beginning. If you thus follow around with a long thong, then untie the original braid and pull it out, you will have the knot of one thong.

Always remember the rule of such knots—you cannot have a number of bights and a number of parts (counting the thongs across) which will have a common divisor.

Thus you can make a Spanish Ring Knot as long as you please, in fact I use them sometimes for wrist loops on quirts and riding crops. As you experiment you will become more and more interested in braiding and thus do your part in keeping alive this old-time cowboy handicraft.

PLATE 5

THE SPANISH RING KNOT

In the previous lesson we have seen how to make the *Spanish Ring Knot* by braiding down five thongs and then joining the ends. This should have given a pretty good idea of the knot.

However, this knot usually is made in a different fashion, in a free-hand way. Only one thong is employed and the completed knot is made with this, but first tying a turk's head and then interweaving.

We will start with a three-part, five-bight turk's head, which is the foundation knot. The mandrel or rounded stick on which it is made has been divided into four areas, so you can tell at a glance when the mandrel has been turned. When you twist the mandrel toward you, or in a clockwise direction, the numbers run from 1 to 4.

The leather thong or rawhide string is laid across the mandrel as shown in *Fig. 1, Plate 5*. The working end is marked "A". It

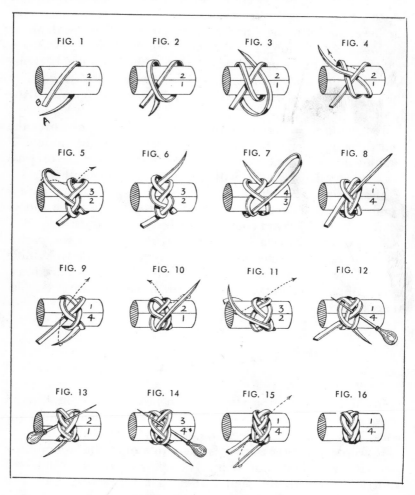

PLATE 5. THE SPANISH RING KNOT

is passed around again over the standing part *(Fig. 2)*; then brought forward and passed beneath the standing part *(Fig. 3)*.

Pay particular attention to *Fig. 4* where the standing part is pulled from beneath that part of the thong to its left. The working end "A" now passes beneath this, as in *Figs.* 5 and 6. In *Fig.* 7 we see the standing part, which was on the left, pulled again beneath the thong to its right (in a way similar to the procedure in *Fig. 4*) and the working end is again passed beneath it. Bring the working end of your thong around and to the front and when it passes up alongside the standing part, the turk's head is complete *(Fig. 8)*.

We begin the woven knot in *Fig. 9*. First withdraw your working end from along the right side of the standing end and pass it over and along to the left side of the standing end *(Fig. 9)*.

In *Fig. 10* it passes over the standing part and then down along to its right side, having gone under the same part of the thong on the edge as did the standing part. In *Fig.* 11 it again passes over the standing part, and up along to the left side of the standing part, having gone under the same part of the thong on the edge that the standing part did.

Now we begin the braid or weave. In *Fig. 12*, the fid shows the path the working end follows, passing beneath two thongs and up, splitting a pair of parallel thongs. On the other side, the working end passes under two thongs and up, splitting two parallel thongs *(Fig. 13)*.

In *Fig. 14* it passes under two and splits two from the other side. It is now brought up alongside the standing end, to its left, after passing under three thongs. *(Fig. 15)*. Completed knot is shown in *Fig. 16*.

Here we have shown a Spanish Ring Knot of over-two under-two sequence. It can be increased to an over-three under-three sequence—or a greater one if desired—by passing the working end around, following the standing part as you did from *Figs.* 9 to 11 inclusive, and then passing around again, splitting the parallel pairs.

This knot will never shake loose or come adrift.

PLATE 6—THE CORE

HOW TO MAKE A RAWHIDE BOSAL

Down in the Mexican State of Sonora they had a habit of breaking a horse when he was young and, so that the bars of his tender mouth might not be injured by a bit, the Mexicans used the *jaquima* (hackamore).

The trick item in hackamore gentling is the *bosal*. It is a noseband of rawhide which has a double function. It serves to cut off the horse's wind when the nose button of the bosal presses against his nose. But, more important, the back or hind part of the bosal in coming up, touches the horse's chin. This teaches the bronc to react.

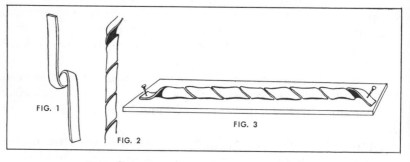

PLATE 6. HOW TO MAKE A RAWHIDE BOSAL—THE CORE

So a bosal, properly fitted, should be rather loose with the front part up, and the lower, or back part, dropping down at an angle. In making a bosal loose it can be adjusted to a smaller size when the *mecate* (McCarty) or reins are attached. The number of wrappings around the lower end determine the tightness of the bosal.

The standard bosal measures twelve inches from the inside of the *nose-button* to the inside of the *heel-knot*. *(Fig. 6, Plate 12)*. Now, in speaking of these things it is best to name the parts of the bosal and how to make it, which is our job.

Most bosals are made on a *core,* either of steel cable or twisted rawhide, whichever is preferred. Some are made without cores. But if made with a core, the core is braided over. This is commonly an 8-string square braid (one with four faces), or on fancier bosals, a 12- or 16-string braid. This core and the braid covering it form the nose-band proper.

In the center of the *nose-band* is the *nose-button,* a long braided knot about seven or eight inches in length. It might be braided over a tapering swell, made by wrapping the nose-band at this point before the nose-button knot is put on. This swell may be made with waxed twine. Sailors call this work "mousing." But many nose buttons do not have this swell or "mouse".

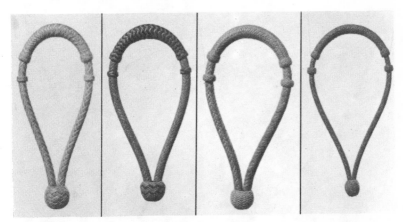

Bosals made by John Conrad, Bellflower, California. Steel cable cores.

On each side of the nose band are one or maybe two side buttons. These serve to hold the headstall in place where it is attached to the nose-band on both sides.

At the point where the nose-band ends come together is the *heel-knot*—a large round, or almost round knot. The heel-knot keeps the ends together, adds some weight to the bosal at this point, and keeps the *fiador* (Theodore) and *mecate* (McCarty) in place. (See illustration of an assembled hackamore, *Fig. 10, Plate 15*).

The first thing is to select your core, if you want one. This may be a piece of telephone guy wire from ⅜ inch to ½ inch in diameter; a four-string piece of braided rawhide; a twisted rawhide core, or a length of braided "spot cord" rope. As the nose-bands of bosals vary from ⅜ inch to 1 inch in diameter, select your core with this in mind. The average bosal nose-band, when the braid is on, is ⅝ inch in diameter.

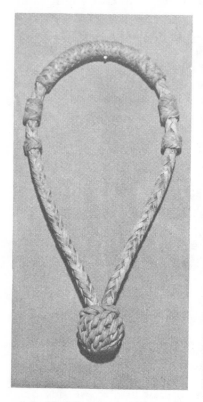
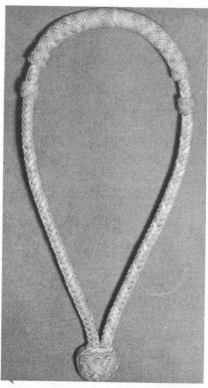

Left: Homemade type of bosal made by L. H. Rutter, Hinsdale, Montana. Very rugged. Nose band braided without core. Note heel knot, made by continuous crowning, like sailors make boat fenders. *Right:* Bosal made by author. Braided over twisted rawhide core. Heel knot is over three, under three braid.

I would say a twisted rawhide core is the best. It should be made from the best of your rawhide. Take a ½ inch strip, two yards in length. Be sure it is the same thickness throughout its length. Then wet it, not too much,—just so it is as pliable as 12-minute spaghetti, with no hard spots in it. Rub in a lot of ordinary yellow laundry soap or saddle soap. The laundry soap is cheaper and just as good.

Now twist the strip upon itself with the *flesh side in* as shown in *Figs. 1* and *2* in *Plate 6*. Twist it until you have thirty-four inches; then pull it and twist it some more until it is tight throughout its entire length. Nail it down by the ends on a board and let it dry *(Fig. 3)*. When it is almost dry place another board on it, or use your foot, and roll it on the board underneath, without moving the nails or loosening it. Roll it back and forth a little. This will smooth it out. Let it remain here a day or so. This is your core.

PLATE 7

EIGHT-STRING SQUARE BRAID OVER CORE

This braid is made over a core. Measure circumference of the core. Divide this by eight. This will give you the width of each string. Say the core is one inch in circumference. Each string will be 1/8 inch wide.

Tie down your strings at one end of the core. Leave about eight inches of strings above the point where you tie down. This is not shown in *Fig. 1, Plate 7,* but is necessary, since these loose strings will later be utilized.

Start braiding as in *Fig. 1*. First bring string *No. 1*, which was on the left side, around to the back, under two strings and over two, to return it to its original side. Arrow-line shows how string No. 8 on the right is brought around to the back and then toward the front, under two and over two.

In *Fig. 2*, the highest string on the left, No. 5, is brought around to the back and forward under two and over two. The arrow-line indicates its path.

Then, on the right, the highest string, No. 6, is carried around to the back and forward under two and over two. Continue in this manner, alternately working the highest string on each side, until you have braided full length of the core.

There should be eight or more inches of free string at this end also, after you have tied down the end of your braid.

There is a shrinkage in braiding. It is well to play safe. Make your strings twice as long as the finished braid.

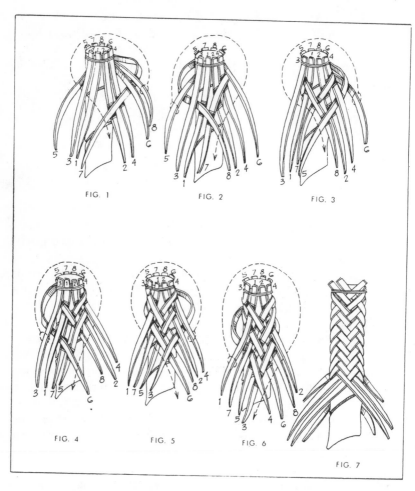

FIG. 1 FIG. 2 FIG. 3

FIG. 4 FIG. 5 FIG. 6 FIG. 7

PLATE 7. HOW TO MAKE A RAWHIDE BOSAL—EIGHT STRING SQUARE BRAID OVER CORE

PLATE 8

EIGHT-STRING SQUARE BRAID WITHOUT CORE

For those who do not use a core,—and I must say I've seen plenty of good bosal nose-bands without cores,—the braid shown in *Fig. 1, 2, 3,* and *4* in *Plate 8* may be used. This is made with eight

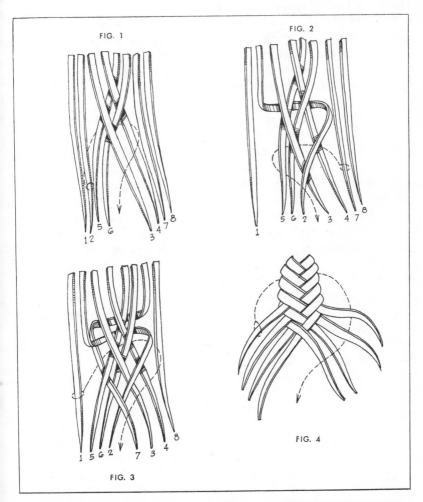

PLATE 8. HOW TO MAKE A RAWHIDE BOSAL—EIGHT STRING SQUARE BRAID WITHOUT CORE

strings, each ¼ inch wide, and, as it is necessary to have some working ends—on both ends of the braid—each string should be about two yards long.

We begin in *Fig. 1*. In this drawing the strings are spread out to better illustrate the sequence. But they should be tied together, leaving about eight inches at the top.

Arrange the four center strings as shown in *Fig. 1*. Then bring string No. 2 around in back and forward over the two front strings, as shown. In *Fig. 2*, the No. 7 string on the right is carried around to the back and then under one and over two, as shown (it actually is under two). In *Fig. 3*, the No. 1 string on the left is carried around back and forward under one (actually under two) and then over two. After this work the upper string on each side alternately, bringing it around in back and then forward under two and over two.

Exert the same even pull on all your strings, and don't let them turn on you, and keep your braid up tight.

Make the braid thirty inches long. Now hang it up with a weight on one end and let it stretch and dry. When it is almost dry, take it down and roll it under your foot on a flat surface; not too hard, but enough to even the braid. This braid has four square faces. Let it dry for a couple of days, with the weight still on it.

When using this braid around a core you can make a 12-string one by coming around under three and then over three; or a 16-string braid by passing under four and over four, or under two, over two, under two, and over two, on each side.

A word again about dampening your strings before using them. Most braiders get their strings too wet. Then, when the braid dries, the strings seem to loosen and show daylight in the work. Have the strings just damp enough so there are no hard spots; then soap them well with laundry soap or saddle soap. Moisten and soap the working ends as they dry out.

PLATE 9

THE NOSE-BUTTON

There still are some old-time rawhide-braiders around. I have located possibly a score or more of them who still are making fancy quirts, bosals, reatas, headstalls and other articles of horse gear. In almost all cases they are "retired" cowboys or buckaroos.

It would not be far-fetched to say that these fellows are the very last of the Old West, survivors of former days, still doing things as they were done in the long ago.

These old-timers have many ingenious tricks in making braided knots. Take the long nose-button knot for a bosal, for instance. There are several ways to make the nose-button knot. One is with a long string of rawhide. The knot is so long, however, that it becomes awkward in working with a lengthy string. A simpler way is with a multiple-string knot, or one which is made by several strings. This is a variation of what I have called later in this book the *"Cowboy Knot"*.

Take a look at *Fig. 1, Plate 9*. You place from three to six strings on the middle part of the nose-band and tie them down the length the finished button is to be,—say eight inches. (Three strings are shown in these drawings for simplicity; you might use more). Make each string about a yard long. The way to determine the width of the string is to: measure the circumference of the nose-band. Say it is one and one-half inches around. In this knot three strings are going to pass back and forth, until they form six bights on each. If you were braiding down, one bight would mean two strings, because you use both ends. So with six bights you are actually using twelve strings. With twelve $1/8$ inch thongs you can cover a circumference of one and one-half inches. So three strings of $1/8$ inch will cover this nose-band. In other words, figure the number of bights or scallops on a woven knot and double it to obtain the actual number of strings you will use.

In winding your strings around the nose-band, as shown in *Fig. 1*, the dress or hair side of the strings is *out*. In *Fig. 3* start your braid. On the left-hand side bring each working end over one string and under one as shown. On the right-hand side bring

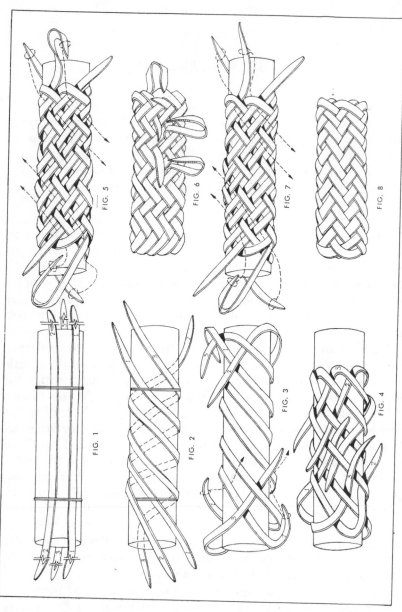

FIG. 1

FIG. 2

FIG. 3

FIG. 4

FIG. 5

FIG. 6

FIG. 7

FIG. 8

PLATE 9. HOW TO MAKE A RAWHIDE BOSAL—THE NOSE-BUTTON

each string under one and over one. These working ends spiral back at right angles to those they pass over and under.

Keep passing over one and under one until the strings from each side meet. You will notice in *Fig. 4* that string No. 1 on the left meets string No. 1 on the right. After the ends of the strings have come together in this fashion, keep working towards the opposite ends, this time doubling the strings.

When you reach the stage shown in *Fig. 5*, bring back the ends on the left under two and over two, splitting the doubled pairs as shown. On the right, the ends come back over two and under two. When the ends meet, as in *Fig. 6*, cut them off and tuck them in the braid. Don't have all pairs of ends coming together in the same part of the knot. Scatter or stagger them so that finished knot is uniform.

This gives you what I call a *"Gaucho Braid"*. The V's in the braid run around the knot. In the next braid *(Fig. 7)*, which I call the *"Herringbone Braid"*, the V's run, or point, the length of the knot.

To make the Herringbone Braid, start back at *Fig. 5*, but pass the working ends as shown in *Fig. 7*. This time the ends on the left go over two and under two. Those on the right go under two and over two. Finished knot is shown in *Fig. 8*.

You may combine these two braids on your nose-button, making it more fancy. On each end make two tucks with the Gaucho Braid, and finish the inside with the Herringbone Braid. Where the two braids join there will be an alternating over-one-under-one sequence, but as this is regular it does not detract from the knot. This makes an attractive button—"very cowboy".

PLATE 10

THE SIDE-BUTTON

Side-buttons on a bosal are for the purpose of holding the hackamore headstall in place and there may be either one or two to a side. If the nose-button is short, make two. The space between the buttons, or between one button and the end of the nose-button is the width of the leather in your hackamore headstall.

The Spanish Ring Knot *(Plate 5)* can be used, but you may like this one better.

I have shown this button worked around a mandrel with a leather collar to better illustrate it. You may work it directly on the nose-band. It is made from one long string, ⅛ inch wide. Play safe and use a string about a yard long. I might add that old-timers work their knots so that there is no need to go back and re-tighten them. This is a good thing to practice and saves string. When you have once properly made your button, it is on good and tight; so you have no need to rework it.

In these drawings the mandrel is numbered on four sides from 1 to 4 clockwise: No. 1 is the front; No. 3 is the back.

Start in *Fig. 1* from the front and pass up and around the mandrel and then back on the right side and up again to go under the standing part. In *Fig. 2*, the working end goes around and then down to the right, over one, and then up to the top where it passes under one and over one.

In *Fig. 3*, the mandrel has been turned slightly to show how, in the third move, the working end passes at the bottom—over one and under one. Then at the top *(Fig. 4)* it is under one, over one, under one.

Fig. 5. Bottom: over one, under one, over one. *Fig. 6*. Top: under one, over one, under one, over one.

Fig. 7 shows the completed skeleton knot, working end coming up alongside the standing end. Braiding of the knot—or turk's head —has started here and it will be seen that the working end passes up on the right of the standing end. At the top it passes under two, bringing it over to the other side of the standing end.

Fig. 8 is the back view. Still following the standing end, the working end passes over it as well as another string and under one to the top.

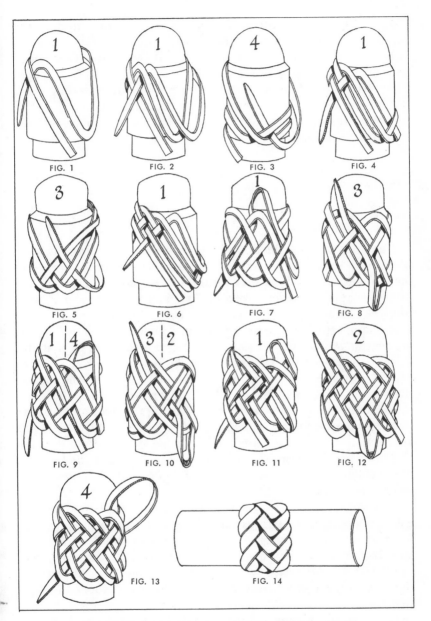

FIG. 1   FIG. 2   FIG. 3   FIG. 4

FIG. 5   FIG. 6   FIG. 7   FIG. 8

FIG. 9   FIG. 10   FIG. 11   FIG. 12

FIG. 13   FIG. 14

PLATE 10. HOW TO MAKE A RAWHIDE BOSAL—THE SIDE-BUTTON

Fig. 9. Top: the sequence is under two, over two, under one.
Fig. 10. Bottom: Over two, under two, over one. *Fig. 11.* Top:
under two, over two, under two. *Fig. 12.* Bottom: over two, under
two, over two. *Fig. 13.* Top: under two, over two, under two.
Then pass around to the front and up alongside standing part.

The completed knot is shown in *Fig. 14.* It can be increased to
over-three-under-three sequence by following around again and
splitting the pairs.

PLATE 11

THE HEEL-KNOT

The final knot on the bosal is the *heel-knot.* But first the ends
of the bosal must be joined together so that the inside measurement, from the inside of nose-button to the point where ends are
joined, is approximately twelve inches. You may want your bosal
longer or shorter—but average size is twelve inches.

In joining the ends together you make a foundation knot. There
are several ways to make this knot. The ends can first be tied and
then secured with the knot shown in *Figs. 9, 10,* and *11* of *Plate
30.* You can use four or six strings, making sure that one half of
them come from each of the ends. This forms a foundation knot.

However, one of the best ways of securing the ends and making
your foundation knot is shown in *Figs. 1* and *2* of *Plate 12.* Ends
are brought together and tied. Then, at the point where they are
tied, you make a *Spanish Ring Knot (Plate 5)* or a *Side-Button
Knot. (Plate 10)* Make either of these knots with a 1/4 inch wide
string and do not make it too tight.

You will recall that, when you braided the nose-band, you left
eight inches of loose strings on each end. Moisten these strings.
Each string is then brought back and through the Ring Knot or
Side Button Knot, as shown in *Fig. 1.* There are sixteen strings
in all and all are passed back and through the knot and pulled
tight. Arrange them in regular order; then cut them off flush
with the knot.

Best covering I know for this foundation knot is one I call the
"Pineapple Knot". It is one of the most practical knots in braiding. As the bights or scallops on each edge are staggered toward

the center, the knot closes on the end when tightened and, in fact, will close on both ends and completely encompass a spherical object. The Pineapple Knot can be interwoven to make it larger, yet its outside bights remain the same in number, enabling it to close over the head of a quirt, bottom of a heel-knot, or other round or semi-round object. It is the King of Braided Knots, and you will find many uses for it. The Argentine Gauchos use it to cover buttons and call it the *Button Knot*.

Take a look at *Plate 11*. We start out by making a four-bight, five-part turk's head, which is completed at *Fig. 7*. This is then raised to a six-bight, seven-part turk's head and is completed at *Fig. 11*. (In case you wish a larger turk's head use the same key in raising it to an eight-bight, nine-part turk's head).

In *Fig. 11* we start braiding or interweaving. (Drawings show this knot made on a mandrel, but you can make it directly on the heel-knot foundation of your bosal). The working end passes along to the right of the standing part, as shown by the arrow-line; and then over to the left under two strings at the point where they cross. In *Fig. 12*, passing down, the working end follows the string on its left. The sequence is over one, under one, over one, under two.

Fig. 13. Going up: over one, under one, over one, under three, splitting parallel strings.

Fig. 14. Going down: over one, under one, over one, under three (splitting two parallel strings).

Fig. 15. Up: over one (not seen in the drawing), under one, over one, under three.

Fig. 16. Down: over two, under one, over one, under three.

Fig. 17. Up: Over two, under one, over one, under three.

Fig. 18. Down: over two, under two, over one, under three.

Fig. 19. Up: over two, under two, over one, under three.

Fig. 20. Down: over two, under two, over two, under three.

Fig. 21. Up: over two, under two, over two, under three.

Fig. 22. Down: over two, under two, over two, under three, which brings the working end up alongside its original starting part. The finished knot is shown in *Fig. 23*, not tightened.

This knot can be made with 1/8-inch strings. If it does not completely cover the foundation knot you will have to enlarge your turk's head, or, better yet, you can enlarge the knot by interweaving in an over-three-under-three sequence. See plate 12.

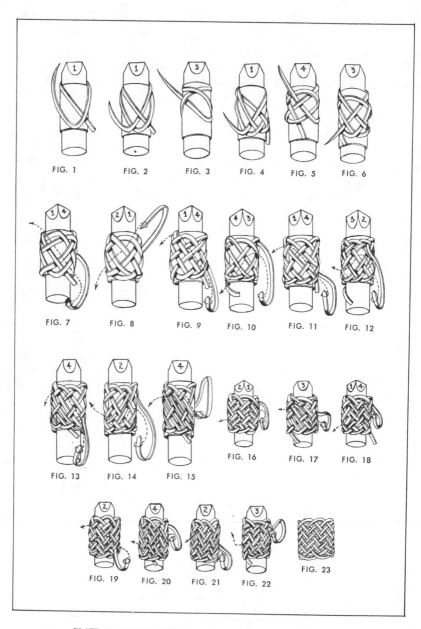

FIG. 1 FIG. 2 FIG. 3 FIG. 4 FIG. 5 FIG. 6

FIG. 7 FIG. 8 FIG. 9 FIG. 10 FIG. 11 FIG. 12

FIG. 13 FIG. 14 FIG. 15 FIG. 16 FIG. 17 FIG. 18

FIG. 19 FIG. 20 FIG. 21 FIG. 22 FIG. 23

PLATE 11. HOW TO MAKE A RAWHIDE BOSAL—THE HEEL KNOT

PLATE 12

THE HEEL-KNOT, cont'd

By using the Pineapple Knot and increasing the sequence you can cover any size foundation knot at the heel of your bosal. For instance, after placing on the over-two-under-two Pineapple Knot detailed in *Plate 11,* you find it does not completely cover the foundation knot, you can go around it again, to make it larger, with an over-three-under-three sequence.

The key to increasing the sequence in this knot is shown in *Figs. 3* and *4, Plate 12.* In *Fig. 3,* the working end which, in the previous explanation, came up alongside its original part, is shown here.

The working end now passes up along on the right of its original part and, at the top, goes under two, as shown by the arrow-line in *Fig. 3.* It now follows down alongside the string above it and then, at the bottom, it passes under four. This is shown by the arrow-line in *Fig. 4.*

In continuing up, the working end passes over two, under two, over two, and under three, splitting two parallel strings in the previous weave.

From this point, the sequence is:

Down: over two, under two, over two, under five, splitting parallel strings.

Up: over two, under two, over two, under three (again splitting two parallel strings).

Down: over three, under two, over two, under five.

Up: over three, under two, over two, under three.

Down: over three, under three, over two, under five.

Up: over three, under three, over two, under three.

Down: over three, under three, over three, under five.

Up: over three, under three, over three, under three.

Down: over three, under three, over three, under five.

This brings the working end alongside the starting portion of the string in this last weave. The knot is complete.

With this key you may increase your knot still more, or, by using a different colored string, produce a contrasting pattern. If you use a different colored string for each interweave you can produce a very fancy knot, indeed.

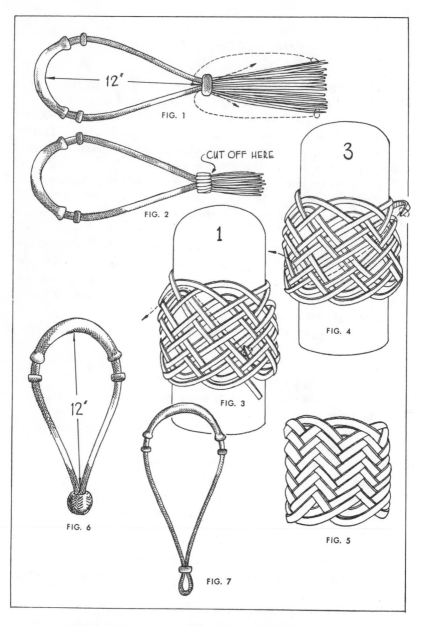

PLATE 12. HOW TO MAKE A RAWHIDE BOSAL—THE HEEL KNOT, *con't*.

I have seen this knot on some old work where it had an over and under sequence of nine,—that is, a string would pass over nine others and under nine.

In *Fig. 6* is shown the completed bosal. The swells at each end of the nose-button are made by placing the nose-button braid over two three-part turk's heads *(Figs. 1 to 8 in Plate 5)*. Swell or taper of the nose-button is made by "mousing," as described in the first part of this explanation of how to make the bosal.

In *Fig. 7* is another type bosal, called a *tie-down bosal*. The core of this is an endless cable and the bosal is usually about pencil-thickness. If made without a core, the ends are spliced together beneath the part covered by the nose-button.

Take your time in making your bosal. The finished product looks difficult, but when you follow each step carefully it is simple. You may work out ideas of your own in the process, as, for example, making the nose-button of leather thongs instead of raw-hide strings.

PLATE 13

HOW TO MAKE A SLIT-BRAID HACKAMORE HEADSTALL

With a knife, some leather, and a little patience, you may make yourself a handsome slit-braid hackamore headstall in a few hours. If you are an expert you can make it in much less time. No metal parts are necessary, and personally, I like this. By using the proper type of braidwork a fellow can do without metal fastenings, buckles, snaps, etc., on any type of horse gear. The gear will be easily adjustable and much more handsome, to my way of thinking. Then there is the satisfaction of. making something in which you need to employ a little ingenuity.

To make your headstall, good strap leather is all right, but what is called "latigo" is better. Real latigo is a vegetable-tanned leather which has been well oiled; but you may use a chrome-tanned latigo. Sometimes you may corral enough good pieces of leather in these so-called repair bundles put up by mail order houses and western outfitters to make yourself a right smart headstall.

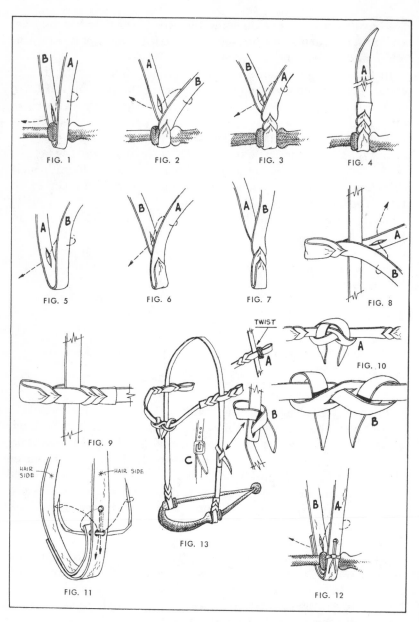

FIG. 1

FIG. 2

FIG. 3

FIG. 4

FIG. 5

FIG. 6

FIG. 7

FIG. 8

FIG. 9

TWIST

FIG. 10

FIG. 11

HAIR SIDE

HAIR SIDE

FIG. 13

FIG. 12

PLATE 13. HOW TO MAKE A SLIT-BRAID HACKAMORE HEADSTALL

You will need four pieces of leather, one-half inch wide and not too thick. One piece will be 18 inches long, another 34 inches, and two 16 inches long.

First take the 34-inch piece, which will form the offside cheek-piece, as well as the headband and part of the nearside cheek-piece. Soak it for a few minutes in water so that it is wet through.

Take a look at *Fig. 1, Plate 13.* Place the leather around offside part of the bosal, between the side-button and the end of the nose-button; or, if your bosal has a couple of side-buttons on each side, place leather around the part of the bosal between the two buttons. In this drawing, the long part of the strap is marked A. The other part, B, should be about six inches long. In B, cut a slit lengthwise and about the width of the leather.

In *Fig. 1* the arrow line shows how A passes through slit in B. Pull it up tight. Now cut a slit in A as shown in *Fig. 2* and pass the end of B through this slit. In *Fig. 3,* A passes through B. *Fig. 4* shows this part of the work completed.

Do the same with the short piece—the one 18 inches long—on nearside of the bosal.

Next we will make the brow-band. Start as in *Fig. 5,* passing B through A, but leaving a loop of about ¾ inch in the leather. Your *fiador,* or throat-latch *(Fig. 10, Plate 15)* passes through this loop.

In *Fig. 6,* A passes through B, shown completed in *Fig. 7.*

The next step is to attach the brow-band to the cheek-piece *(Fig. 8).* Here B passes through A and then A through B, and, finally, B through A again. The work will look like the drawing in *Fig. 9.* You may make it all a little more fancy with additional slit-braid work, but be sure your straps are longer because there is some shrinkage in this braid.

Attach your brow-band on the other side. *Fig. 10* shows two ways of joining these two brow-band pieces in the center so that they are adjustable.

In this type of slit-braiding the flesh side shows in alternate braids. To obtain a more finished braid where only the hair or dress side is out, make your cheek-pieces as in *Fig. 11.* Here two pieces of leather are joined together with a 3-hole fastening. In *Fig. 12,* it will be shown that A passes through two thicknesses of leather and secures the other end of the splice.

If you observe *Fig. 13* at the drawing marked A, you will see how to obtain a similar finished braid on the brow-band. The loop is

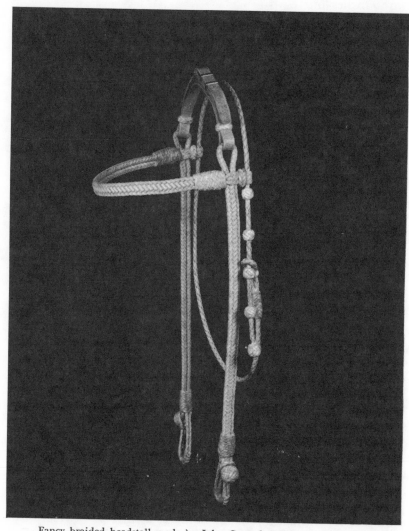

Fancy braided headstall made by John Conrad, Bellflower, California.

formed by holding the leather together with a turk's head or Spanish Ring Knot (*Plate 5*). Then, behind the cheek-piece, the leather is given a twist so the hair side will be *out* in both pieces.

The completed headstall is shown in *Fig. 13*. A slit is made in the end of the long cheek-piece and the shorter one passes through it to form the knot you see there. This makes the headstall adjustable. If you are a gadget man you may use a buckle here.

PLATE 14

HOW TO MAKE A BRAIDED HACKAMORE HEADSTALL

A fancier headstall than that just described can be made entirely of braid. By the use of woven knots it is made adjustable to fit any horse's head. Such a headstall is used with a pencil-width bosal.

This headstall (*Fig. 14, Plate 14*) consists of the following parts:

1 metal ring 1⅜ inches outside measurement, covered with braidwork (Marked A in *Fig. 14*).

2 long braided "rounds" 40 inches each for the offside cheek-piece, head-piece, and part of the nearside cheek-piece. (B).

1 braided "round" 24 inches for the lower part of nearside cheek-piece. (C).

2 braided "rounds" 26 inches each for the brow-band. (D).

Woven knots of various sizes.

This headstall can be made with a four-string braid, illustrated in *Plate 30*, with or without a *core*. If used with a core, this core should be braided cord. The eight-string braid shown in *Plate 7* can be used over a core. Measure circumference of the core and then divide this by the number of strings to be used in your braid. The result will give you the width of each string. For example, if the core is an inch in circumference and you use eight strings, each string will be ⅛ inch in width.

When latigo or leather thongs are used it is best to employ a core. If you use rawhide strings, no core will be necessary and the best braid for this purpose is shown in *Plate 8*—the eight-string braid.

With or without the core, make your thongs or strings about double the length of finished braid to take care of shrinkage,

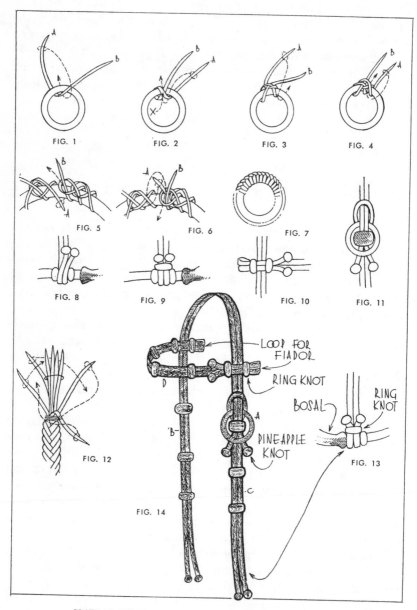

FIG. 1

FIG. 2

FIG. 3

FIG. 4

FIG. 5

FIG. 6

FIG. 7

FIG. 8

FIG. 9

FIG. 10

FIG. 11

FIG. 12

LOOP FOR FIADOR

RING KNOT

BOSAL

RING KNOT

PINEAPPLE KNOT

FIG. 13

FIG. 14

PLATE 14. HOW TO MAKE A BRAIDED HACKAMORE HEADSTALL

and leave enough unbraided on each end to tie a foundation knot for your covering or woven knot.

We will start with the metal ring. In *Fig. 1* is shown the first step in covering this with a Spanish type edge-braid of two loops. The end B should be about two inches long. Working end A is passed through the ring as shown, and then brought forward over B and through the ring once more. In *Fig. 2*, the working end A is brought back and passed beneath the crossed strings X, and between the strings and the outer rim of the ring. The working end in this instance does not pass through the ring.

In *Fig. 3*, the working end passes through the ring and, in *Fig. 4*, is brought back, once more beneath the crossed strings,—but not through the ring. Braid is continued in this manner until it covers the ring and is near the starting point.

To join the braid after it has been made around ring, look at *Fig. 5*. Standing end B has been pulled out as shown. Working end A passes through the ring and up in back through the same loop which contains B. The working end A next passes underneath two crossed strings and then down through the loop containing B, through which A previously passed. Now draw your braid tight and cut off ends A and B flush with the braid.

In our drawings the braid is shown very loose, so that details can be more easily followed. The covered ring is shown in *Fig. 7*.

In *Fig. 12* is shown how the ends are tied for the foundation knot. Four strings are used for this purpose. Details of this knot are shown in *Figs. 9* and *10, Plate 30*, or you may use the knot shown in *Figs. 9, 10, 11,* and *12* in *Plate 31*. Cut your ends off flush with the top of the knot.

The woven knot which covers this foundation knot is the *Pineapple Knot,* shown in *Plate 11*. The Pineapple Knot is used also in the other woven knots shown on the finished headstall. However, the Spanish Ring Knot *(Plate 5)* is best for the smaller knots on the brow-band and those fastening the cheek-pieces to the bosal.

The knot at the point of adjustment on the nearside cheek-piece should be smaller than the inside of the metal ring.

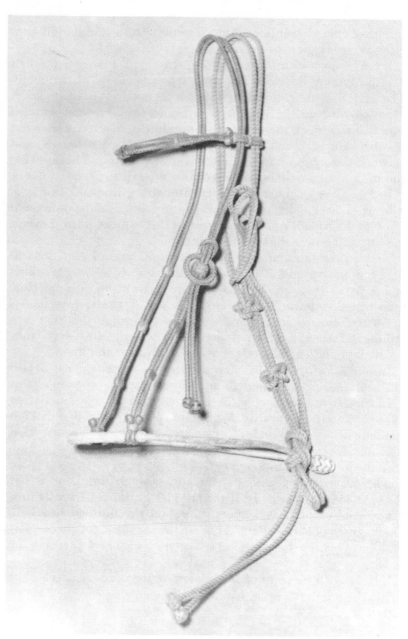

Completely rigged hackamore made by Duff Severe, Pendleton, Oregon. Braided headstall, pencil type bosal.

PLATE 15

RIGGING THE HACKAMORE

The Western *hackamore* pretty well illustrates the influence of the Mexican *vaquero* on the American cowboy and buckaroo. Not only is the idea of its use Mexican —and we mean *Mexican* as adapted from the Spanish *conquistadores,*—all names for parts of the hackamore coming in a picturesque jargon from the Mexican.

Hackamore originally was *jáquima* (hah'-key-mah). The cowboy twisted it around to suit himself and when he got through with the word it was "hackamore". The bosal comes from *bozal* and so has remained almost in its pure form. The "Theodore" and "Theodore Knot" come from the word *fiador* (fee'-ah-dohr). Many believe this safety device, or throat-latch, with its intricate knot got its name from *Theodore Roosevelt,* but, considering the liberties the cowboy took with other Spanish and Mexican words, he undoubtedly merely converted *fiador* into "Theodore". Then there is the *mecate* (may-kah'-tay), or hair rope used as reins and lead-rope. The cowboy calls this "McCarty".

The hackamore, and I call it this to mean headstall, fiador, bosal and mecate, is handy gear around a ranch or any place where horses need to be gentled. Its use is one of the oldest in breaking horses and has long been popular in the West, particularly in California. Others more expert than myself can explain the value of the hackamore method in teaching a horse to neck rein.

We have made the different parts of the hackamore, namely, the *headstall* and the *bosal,* so now it must be properly rigged.

The first thing is to make the *double hackamore knot*. It is interesting how writers on knots and rope work have explained the hackamore knot as used by the cowboy. They claim that this knot —also known as the *bag, bottle, jug,* and *beggarman's knot*—after being made, may be loosened up and used as a sort of halter, or headstall. Let us forget all this nonsense and see just how the hackamore knot is actually fashioned and used.

First, it must be tied double. Take fourteen or fifteen feet of good braided cord—No. 10 Sampson spot rope that resembles clothesline is the best. Double it. About three feet from the bight marked A in *Fig. 1, Plate 15,* start your knot by laying it out as

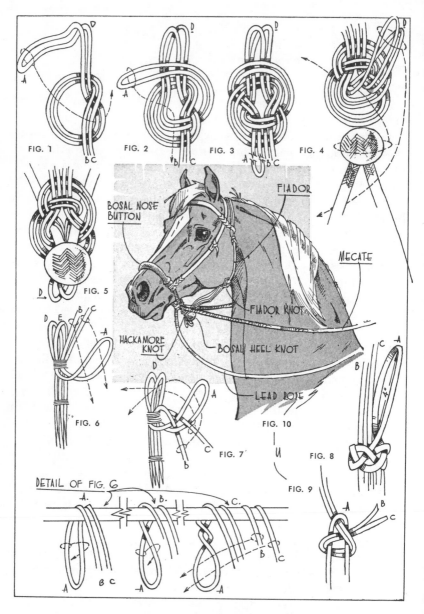

FIG. 1

FIG. 2

FIG. 3

FIG. 4

FIG. 5

FIG. 6

FIG. 7

FIG. 8

FIG. 9

FIG. 10

DETAIL OF FIG. 6

BOSAL NOSE BUTTON

FIADOR

MECATE

HACKAMORE KNOT

FIADOR KNOT

BOSAL HEEL KNOT

LEAD ROPE

PLATE 15. RIGGING THE HACKAMORE

shown. Follow the arrowline in *Fig. 1;* then follow the arrowline in *Fig. 2.* Straighten out your rope carefully so that it does not overlap in the knot and leaves about two inches of the double bight D above the knot. Bight A below the knot should be about eighteen inches in length.

This is the knot that secures the lower end of the fiador to the bosal. In *Fig. 4,* it will be noted that the knot is loosened and the double bight D has been withdrawn. Through the space, push the nose-button of the bosal, as shown by the arrowline. Then bring bight D down through the space between the nose-band and back through the loops in the knot it formerly occupied. Tighten it as shown in *Fig. 5,* leaving two inches of bight D below.

The *fiador knot* is started about six inches above the double hackamore knot. Remember there were two ends, marked B and C, and the bight marked A. These are tied together as shown in *Fig. 6,* bight A being turned down to form the two bights, D and E.

The secret of making this knot is the twist given to bight A, when it is brought forward beneath the part where it is tied. To better illustrate this I have shown the steps in this twist in *Figs. 11, 12,* and *13.* Be sure to arrange the rope in this fashion in tying the knot according to the diagrams in *Figs. 6* and *7.*

Bight A should be about 4 inches long when the knot is completed (*Fig. 8*). In tightening the knot after *Fig. 7,* seize the ends B and C and the bight A, remove the tie-string, and work the knot until it looks as in *Fig. 8.* Its position on the fiador is seen in *Fig. 10.* In *Fig. 9* is the simple knot used to fasten the ends of the fiador.

PLATE 16

THAT "OLE" FIADOR KNOT

The *fiador* is the toughest of all horse gear knots to tie. While instructions to make it are given in the previous chapter, still many letters have come from readers who say they have found it impossible to tie the fiador.

Possibly more cuss words have been wasted on this "ole" fiador knot than on all the one-cow stampeding Brahmas, balky jack-asses and ornery bronco gizzard-poppers and gut-twisters put together.

The fiador, or Theodore, can almost be labelled "the knot that nobody can tie." Of course, there still are some old-timers who can whip up this knot, and some have their own private way of doing it. But even these fellows are getting scarcer and scarcer, and that is too bad, because the fiador is the one typically horseman's knot. Most all other knots can be traced to sailors and sail-

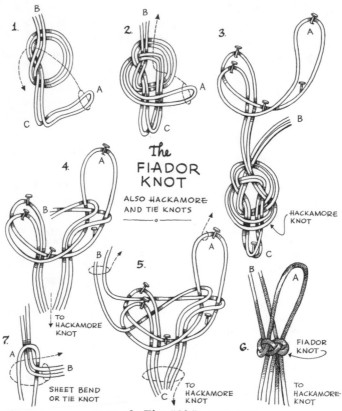

The FIADOR KNOT

ALSO HACKAMORE AND TIE KNOTS

PLATE 16. *That "Ole"* FIADOR KNOT

ing ships—but not the fiador. It came hundreds of years ago from the Argentine Pampas and up through Mexico and into the Southwest—and it came on horses and not on ships.

Today, a very small percentage of the horsemen who use the hackamore with the fiador tie this classic knot themselves—either it comes with the rig when they buy it, or they purchase it from a saddle shop or mail order house with the knot already tied. Should these riders transfer the fiador from one hackamore to another, they are careful not to upset or capsize the knot.

So, for those who want to tie the fiador to *use* it, or those who simply want to learn to make it for the satisfaction of helping to keep alive a part of the Old West, we believe a simple, foolproof way has been worked out.

In showing how the fiador is made, we have also described again the making of the two other knots that go with it—the hackamore knot, which secures the heel knot of the bosal, and the sheet bend or tie knot, by which the fiador is adjusted and fastened. By doing all the knots together, their relationship to each other can be illustrated more clearly.

The hackamore knot should be made first. Take 15 feet of sash cord and middle it, forming the loop or bight A in *Fig. 1*. With 3 feet of the doubled cord—from B to A in *Fig. 1*—start the knot as shown, working with the loop A. In *Fig. 2* the final pass is made as indicated by the arrow-line. The double bight C at the bottom should be about 2 inches. The bight A should extend above the knot about 13 inches, as this will be a part of the fiador knot.

Now, take a board and hammer and six nails (*Fig. 3*). The distance between the bottom nail and the top nail should be about 1 foot, and between those on the right and those on the left, about ½ foot. You don't have to be too exact about placing the nails, as they are merely to hold the rope turns apart.

Secure loops C of the hackamore knot over the lower nail. Then, working with loop A as shown in *Fig. 3*, pass it around the nails, as shown, being careful about crossing the strands, and finally loop it over the top nail. Next, work the two ends marked B as shown in *Fig. 4*. Complete the knot as shown in *Fig. 5*. Take the loop A and the ends B in one hand and the loops C in the other and remove the rope from the nails and draw the hands apart, tightening the knot. With a little coaxing, the fiador knot will emerge as shown in *Fig. 6*.

The fiador knot should be about 6 inches above the hackamore knot, but this must be adjusted to suit the horse's head. The manner of making the tie knot is shown in *Fig. 7*.

Some expert fiador knot makers may grumble that this "ain't the right way" to tie this knot, but, "what the hackamore!"—the result is the same.

PLATE 17

THE HACKAMORE REINS AND LEAD-ROPE KNOT

The hackamore reins and lead-rope are made from one long twisted *horse hair* rope, known in Mexico as the *mecate*. As with other horse gear terms from below the Border, the cowboy has changed this to suit himself. He calls it *McCarty*.

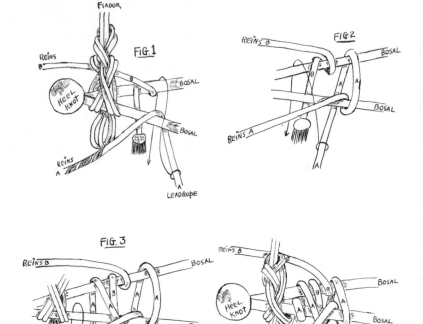

PLATE 17. THE HACKAMORE REINS AND LEAD-ROPE KNOT

The *mecate* is twenty-two feet long and varies from three-eighths of an inch to five-eighths of an inch in diameter. Some are three-quarters of an inch in diameter.

At one end of the *mecate* is a tassel known as *la mota*.

The first step is to determine the length of the reins. This is usually done by holding the bosal knot and the doubled *mecate* in one hand and then stretching the other hand out to form a bight which will be the reins. This measurement is termed a *brazada*, or the distance from hand to hand when the arms are extended. Another way is to place a bight of the *mecate* in the saddle seat and measure to the position of the bosal heel knot— both bosal and saddle on the horse, of course.

In *Fig. 1* is shown a portion of the bosal with the hackamore knot tied. The hackamore reins and lead-rope knot is tied just forward of the hackamore knot. Take that portion of the *mecate* with the *mota*, or tassel, and wrap it around the left cheek of the bosal, as shown. This section of the *mecate* is marked B. Take the other section, marked A, and lay it over the right cheek of the bosal, as shown.

The arrow-line indicates the next turn of A.

In *Fig. 2,* the previous turns are shown, with the arrow-line showing the next turn of that section, marked A. Notice the turn is made beneath the reins.

In *Fig. 3,* the final turns are made, as indicated by the arrow-line. Notice that A, which is the lead-rope, passes through the two bights of the hackamore knot. *Fig. 4* shows the completed knot. It is loose and should be pushed up snug against the hackamore knot.

More turns can be taken with section A, if desired. By these turns, the bosal can be adjusted to fit the horse.

The inside measurement of the bosal from the heel knot to the nose button usually is twelve inches. This is the size you will receive from a dealer if you do not specify a definite measurement. If you build the bosal yourself for a particular horse, you will of course make it to fit that horse's head.

The turns taken with section A as described above close the sides of the bosal near the heel knot. Thus if your bosal is too large for the horse upon which it is to be used, you take a sufficient number of turns to close it up at this point and thereby reduce it in size However, the bosal should not fit snugly, but loose enough so that the heel knot drops well below the plane of the nose button. Take great care to adjust your bosal correctly.

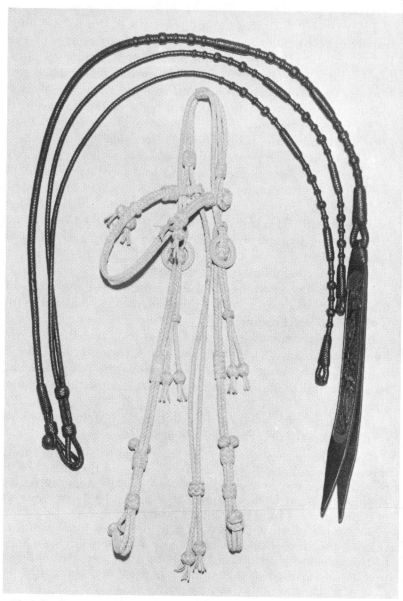

Black leather reins and romal made by Ernie Ladouceur of Madera, California. White rawhide headstall made by the author to specifications in this book. Buttons are interwoven with a darker shade of rawhide.

PLATE 18

HOW TO MAKE A BRAIDED BRIDLE HEADSTALL

If a horse could laugh, he would express much amusement over some of the baubles and gaudy trinkets his owner puts on bridles, saddles, and other riding gear.

Still, the average animal does not appear too happy about this heavy, out-of-character "horse jewelry". Many of them seem downright sad, especially when they are carrying a saddle that requires two men to place into position, or wear a bridle bearing all sorts of metal do-dads that would weigh down any proud horse's head.

A few expensive and carefully selected conchas and buckles may not be out of place on ordinary occasions, and perhaps a horse *diked* out like a dowager at the opening night of the opera is *de rigueur* in a parade or on a movie set, but for my part I like leather carving, saddle-stamping, and braidwork as decoration for horse-gear at all times.

A decorative bridle headstall can be made entirely of braidwork. No metal fastenings of any kind are needed. If you want it particularly fancy you may use several colors in your rawhide strings or leather thongs.

This bridle headstall is similar to the braided hackamore headstall with the exception that there are two cheek-headpiece adjustments instead of one—one on each side—a throat-latch, and cheek-bit loops. Here are the specifications:

	Length when braided	Number and width of strings	Length of each string	Total
Throat-latch (1)	4 ft. 6 in.	8 3/32 in.	9 ft.	72 ft.
Brow-band (2)	2 ft. 2 in.	16 3/32 in.	5 ft.	80 ft.
Head-piece (2)	2 ft. 6 in.	16 1/8 in.	5 ft.	80 ft.
Cheek-piece (2)	3 ft.	16 1/8 in.	6 ft.	96 ft.
Cheek-Bit Loop (2)	9 in.	16 1/8 in.	18 in.	24 ft.
				352 ft.

There will be some twenty-eight buttons, or woven knots, which will require an additional 84 feet of string. So the grand total for making this headstall will be about 436 feet of rawhide string.

The braiding will be the 8-string square, as shown in *Plate 8*. In case you use leather thongs, and braid over a core of braided rope, use the braid shown in *Plate 7*.

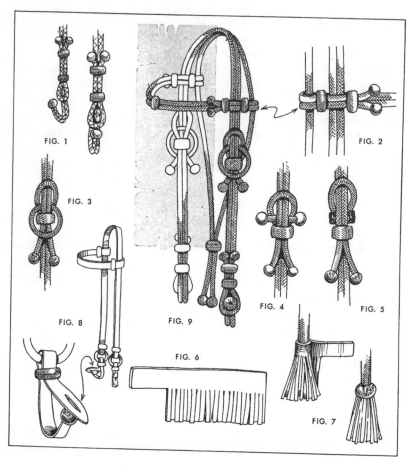

PLATE 18. HOW TO MAKE A BRAIDED BRIDLE HEADSTALL

Follow the instructions for making the braided hackamore headstall, only in this case use two braid-covered metal rings instead of one, and also make your throat-latch and cheek-bit loops. *(Fig. 1)* In making the latter, the cheek-piece ends are first joined together with a foundation knot *(Figs. 9-12, Plate 30)*, then covered with a woven knot. *(Plate 11)*

There are several ways of making the headpiece-cheekpiece adjustment. One is with metal rings as shown in *Fig. 3;* another is by braiding over a short, stiff piece of rawhide and placing a button on each end, as shown in *Fig. 4.* In *Fig. 5,* there is neither the ring nor the crosspiece, and the adjustment is made with two woven buttons or knots as shown.

If you wish to make a bridle head from strap leather, follow the details in *Fig. 9.*

The *cheek-bit loop* is made from strap leather also. On one end cut four thongs, cutting back several inches. Then make a foundation knot as shown in *Figs. 9* and *10, Plate 30,* or in *Figs. 9, 10, 11* and *12, Plate 31.* Cover this with the Pineapple Knot (*Plate 11*). The ring knot which holds the loop to the ring is slipped down close to the button, where it passes through the slit in the leather and holds it in place.

When using leather thongs the ends can be finished off with *tassels,* or, as the cowboy says, "frills". Cut your frill as shown in *Fig. 6* and then wrap it around the end of the "round". Sew it and lash it. Then cover with a Pineapple Knot.

PLATE 19

HOW TO MAKE A PAIR OF BRAIDED REINS

Reins are of two general types,—*open* and *closed.* In the old days the Texas cowboy favored open reins, while the California buckaroo was partial to closed reins.

The open ones are not joined together at the saddle-end, so, if the rider is thrown, he is in no danger of becoming entangled in them. Also, when a horse is grazing, his reins would not get caught in the brush. But the chief point was that, when the cowboy dismounted, he merely let his reins drop to the ground, so that, if the horse tried to get away, the animal would step on the reins' ends and stop himself.

Closed reins usually have a long flexible quirt, or *romal,* attached at the saddle-end (*Plate 22*).

If using leather thongs in making your reins, I suggest that a core be used. In such case measure around the core and divide this measurement by eight—if using eight thongs. Thus if a core measures one inch in circumference, use eight ⅛-inch thongs. Core should be of braided rope, 9 feet long. Thongs should be twice that length.

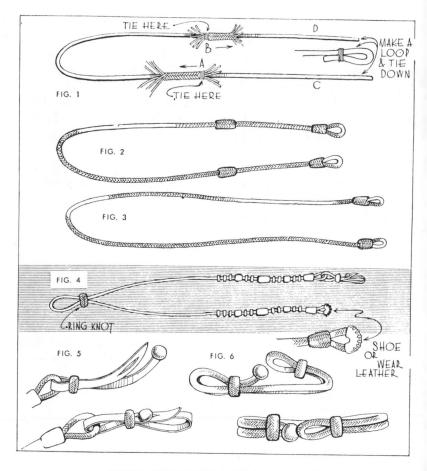

PLATE 19. HOW TO MAKE A PAIR OF BRAIDED REINS

Braiding with leather or latigo thongs will be slightly different than with rawhide. With leather thongs, braid the middle part of your closed reins as shown in *Fig. 1,* starting braid at A and finishing at B. Then braid the two sections from A to C and from B to D. This break may be wrapped tightly with waxed twine and then covered with a braided knot. (*Fig. 2.*)

Open reins may be braided in the same manner. The approximate length of these is 7 feet.

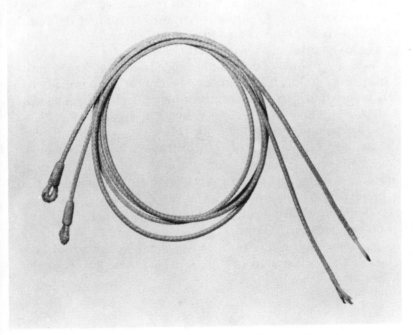

Open reins braided by John Conrad, Bellflower, California.

Rawhide reins usually are braided in their entirety. That is, there is no break in the braid. If the completed reins are to be 9 feet long use eight ⅛-inch strings, each 18 feet in length. No core is necessary. Use the 8-string braid shown in *Plate 8*.

Rawhide reins are shown in *Fig. 3*. Turn back each end to form a loop about 1 inch long. Lash down the ends and cover this part with the "Cowboy Knot" shown in *Plate 21*.

You may scatter as many knots along the lower ends of these reins as you desire. But be sure you have the same number and same kinds on each side. Larger knots may be the Cowboy Knot

(Plate 18) or the Pineapple Knot *(Plate 11)*; smaller ones, the Ring Knot *(Plate 5)*; or the Bosal Side-button Knot. *(Plate 10)*

In *Fig. 4* is shown the way they can be placed. In the old days when horsemen used a "Spade Bit" or a heavy "Mexican Bit", these knots served a purpose. They covered weights for balancing such bits—wicked instruments in unpracticed hands.

In either the leather or rawhide reins a braid-covered ring *(Plate 14)* about 1 inch in outside diameter can be enclosed in the loops on the ends of the reins. Chains are then used to connect the reins to the bit. Such chains prevent a horse from working the reins' ends around to his mouth and chewing on them.

However, a *rein-bit fastener* can be made from a leather or rawhide strap *(Fig. 5)*. The button-knot on end of the strap is made by slitting it into four parts and then forming an end knot, as shown in *Plate 30*. This knot can be covered by a Pineapple Knot. *(Plate 11)* The "keeper knot" is a Ring Knot. *(Plate 5)*

A more fancy rein-bit fastener can be made of braided rawhide. *(Fig. 6)* You will, of course, need two such fasteners, and each should be braided 9 inches long. This braid is then doubled, the ends braided into a single knot *(Figs. 9-12, Plate 31)*, and then covered with the Pineapple Knot. *(Plate 11)* Now place two ring knots on each fastener, as shown.

Loops on the ends of the reins can be fitted with wear-leathers or shoes. This is illustrated in *Fig. 4*. Such a wear-leather is the same as that detailed in *Plate 30*.

PLATE 20

HOW TO SECURE REIN KNOTS

Small knots which are made on braided reins and braided quirts are spaced an exact distance apart and they should remain that way during the life of the article. However, when such knots are made with one string, it is difficult to keep them in place, however tightly they may be braided.

In *Fig. 1* is shown the start of a simple knot made on a four-string round braid. As can be seen, the standing parts of the strings are first inserted beneath the braid. The working ends of the strings are crowned clockwise, as indicated by the arrow-lines.

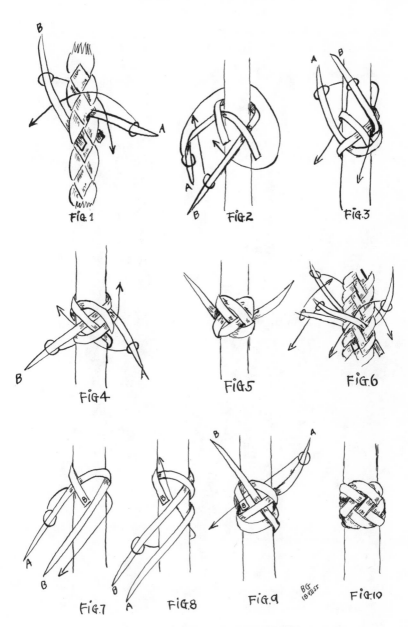

FIG. 1 FIG. 2 FIG. 3

FIG. 4 FIG. 5 FIG. 6

FIG. 7 FIG. 8 FIG. 9 FIG. 10

PLATE 20. HOW TO SECURE REIN KNOTS

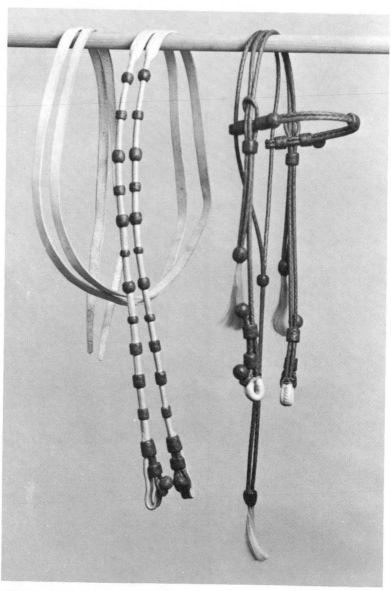

Black leather braided headstall and white leather reins made by Burt Rogers, Spearfish, South Dakota. The headstall has white horsehair tassels and the reins are decorated with black braided leather buttons.

In *Fig.* 2, the strings are crowned in reverse, as shown by the arrow-lines. Next, in *Fig.* 3, the two working ends, A and B, pass under two, and in *Fig.* 4, have passed over two and now upward under two The knot is completed. The ends are cut off. This knot will not slip.

In *Fig.* 6 is shown the beginning of the same knot on an eight-string braid. Four strings are used here, but the sequence of each string is the same as that of the previous knot.

A knot of the "Head-hunter" variety is shown in the next sequence. The braid around which the knot is made is not shown, but the ends are inserted here as before explained.

In *Fig.* 7, the strings have been crowned. The arrow-line shows how string A is brought around and parallel to string B. In *Fig.* 8, string B is now passed around and over A and under its own part, as shown by the arrow-line.

String A passes up over one, under one. (Not shown)

Next, in *Fig.* 9, string A passes down under two, over two (one being the standing part B), and under one. String B passes down under two, over two (one being the standing part A) and under one. In the next sequence (not shown) string A passes up over two and under two alongside the standing part B. String B passed up over two and under two alongside the standing Part A.

This is an attractive knot of over two-under two sequence, and, though made of but two strings, it has four bights. The finished knot is shown in *Fig.* 10.

PLATE 21

THE SHORT COWBOY KNOT—GAUCHO WEAVE

Now and then a knot turns up which demonstrates the ingenuity of old-time braiders. Such a knot is the one I have named the "Cowboy Knot". I have never heard it called that, in fact I have never heard it given any name but "knot", or possibly "multiple-string knot". So, as likewise with many other braids and woven knots, I have taken it upon myself to give this knot a "handle".

The knot can be made with one long string or thong. In my book *Leather Braiding,* I have shown how to make the knot that way and termed it the "Double Gaucho Knot of Two Passes".

The advantage of making it with several strings—especially when working with rawhide—is that the braider can work the knot tight from the start and there is little adjustment to be made after it is woven. Then, too, shorter strings being used, there is no need of continually pulling one long string through the knot as the work progresses.

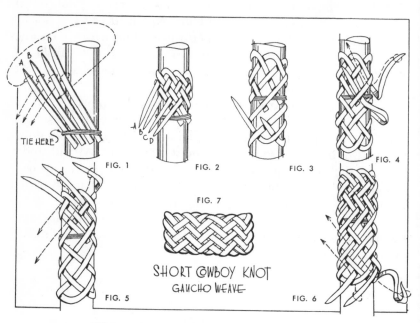

PLATE 21. THE SHORT COWBOY KNOT—GAUCHO WEAVE

While I have specifically labeled this "The Short Cowboy Knot", it can be made any length. Thus it can be used in fashioning the nose-button on a bosal and for many other purposes.

In *Fig. 1* the knot is started with four strings or thongs. You may use as many as you like—I have simply used four by way of illustration. These strings are tied down at the standing ends, as shown, the flesh side against the core.

I might add here that more experienced braiders do not tie down these ends. They simply hold them down with the thumb

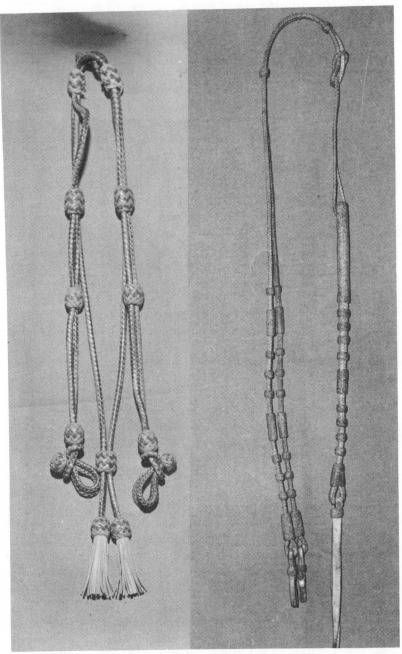

Left: Braided ear-head made by author. *Right:* Fancy braided reins and romal made by Tom Dorrance, Joseph, Oregon.

until secured as the braid progresses. The former method, however, is recommended for the beginner.

The next step, indicated by the arrowlines in *Fig. 1,* is to "crown" all the working ends. This means that each end passes beneath the thong to its left. Thong D passes beneath Thong C; Thong C beneath Thong B; Thong B beneath Thong A, and Thong A passes around the back of the core and to the front under Thong D.

The crown is tightened and the tied-down ends are then adjusted so they are evenly spaced around the core. Sequence is the basket-weave, or over one, under one. This is shown in *Fig. 2.*

After the thongs have been passed under one, over one, under one, over one, you spiral or wrap them down for the length you wish the knot. In this case they have been wrapped around once.

In *Fig. 3* you start working from the bottom. If you turned the work upside down, you would see that you "crown" the thongs again. If it is held upright, the term is to "wall" them. Anyway, each thong at the bottom passes beneath the one to its left. It is then brought up, over one, under one, until it meets the standing end (the tied-down part). Each thong will systematically come out at the proper place; that is, will join with the proper standing end. By this I mean that it should meet it in such a way that you can parallel it on the right side. *(Fig. 4)*

In *Fig. 5,* all working ends have been brought to the top and each is on the right-hand side of its standing end. Then, as shown in *Fig. 5* by the arrow-lines, the working end passes down under two. Each working end brought to the top makes this same pass. Parallel thongs, or pairs, are split by the working end as it proceeds downward. Then it begins to follow parallel to the thong on its left to the bottom of the knot.

At the bottom, *(Fig. 6)* each working end is brought up under two at the edge. Working ends are then passed upward in an over-two-under-two sequence, splitting the parallel pairs until they join the over-two-under-two sequence at the top. The knot is now finished. Ends are cut off and tucked. The finished braid is shown in *Fig. 7.*

This produces a braid where the V's point around the circumference of the knot. I term this a "gaucho weave". The "herringbone weave", in which V's point toward the ends of the knot is illustrated in same class of knot in *Plate 23.*

It might be added that a knot 1 inch long can be made with four ⅛-inch strings each 10 inches long. This would give a finished knot with 13 parts and 8 bights or scallops.

PLATE 22

HOW TO MAKE A BRAIDED ROMAL

The *romal*—ramal, or romel, as it is sometimes written—is a long flexible quirt or whip attached to the saddle-end of closed reins. This romal is about 3 feet in length with a lash of 10 inches or more.

In *Fig. 1* is shown a fancy romal, with knots scattered along its lower end, and a braided lash. This is a type made by John Conrad, of Bellflower, California. It may be made without the decorative knots and braided lash, its utility value being thus unaffected.

To make the romal, take four ⅛-inch wide rawhide strings, each 12 feet long. Middle them and at this point work them into a 4-string round braid (*Plate 28*), sufficient for the loop shown at the top of the romal. Now bring the eight strings together and braid them down in an 8-string braid without core (*Plate 8*) for 3 feet 6 inches. This will give you enough at the bottom for turning braid back to form an eye or loop. Braid is lashed down where the eye is formed and this part covered with a woven knot.

You have a variety of woven knots from which to choose in decorating your romal. In *Plate 23* is shown the Cowboy Button Knot, which may be used for the longer knots at the top and bottom of the romal and that in the center of the other knots along its lower end. The braided lash is detailed in *Plate 24*.

To attach the romal to the reins you can use either of the two types of fastenings shown in *Figs. 2* or *3*. The one in *Fig. 2* is illustrated more fully in *Plate 19*.

In *Fig. 3* the fastening is made directly on the end of the romal. A short length is braided and a button worked on the end. This is lashed to the end of the romal as shown. The loop for the button is made by turning back the end of the romal and lashing it down; then covering it with a woven knot. However, in an 8-string braid, you can make two 4-string braids into the button and loop ends.

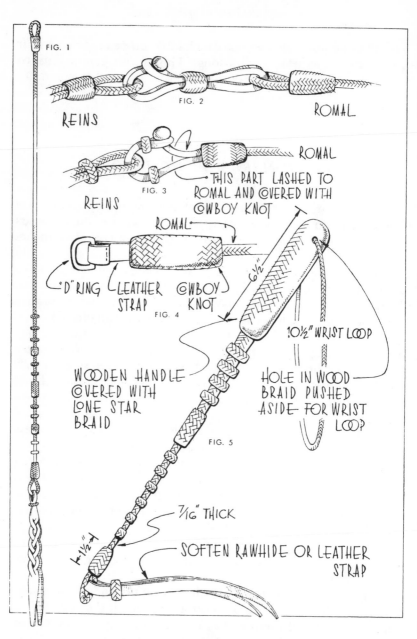

FIG. 1

FIG. 2

REINS

ROMAL

FIG. 3

REINS

ROMAL

THIS PART LASHED TO ROMAL AND COVERED WITH COWBOY KNOT

ROMAL

"D" RING

LEATHER STRAP

COWBOY KNOT

FIG. 4

6½"

10½" WRIST LOOP

WOODEN HANDLE COVERED WITH LONE STAR BRAID

HOLE IN WOOD BRAID PUSHED ASIDE FOR WRIST LOOP

FIG. 5

7/16" THICK

1½"

SOFTEN RAWHIDE OR LEATHER STRAP

PLATE 22. HOW TO MAKE A BRAIDED ROMAL

If a D-ring fastening is desired, it can be made as shown in *Fig. 4*. Here the D-ring is slipped through a strap lashed to the braided end of the romal. It is shown stitched down in the illustration, but it is better to bring the end back and lash it down on the romal end, covering it, of course, with a woven knot. Types shown in *Figs. 3* and *4* are used by Duff Severe of Pendleton, Oregon.

In *Fig. 5* is shown a romal sent me by Tom Dorrance, of Joseph, Oregon. The handle is made of a round piece of wood, 6½ inches long and ⅞ inch in diameter. A hole is bored up in its lower end into which the braid is slipped and secured by pegs or nails driven in crosswise. Handle is covered with a long woven knot. This may be the Cowboy Button Knot with Pineapple-knot weave, as explained in the text with *Plate 23*. Such a braid will close on the top of the handle. Or you may use the "Lone Star Knot", shown in *Plate 28*.

Near the top of the handle a hole is bored through. Braid on the handle is pushed aside and a wrist loop of 4-string braid is passed through it. The place where the ends of the braid are tied together is worked into the hole.

This romal has a slight taper. The body is made of a 12-string braid (see text with *Plate 8*). In this case your strings are cut to a taper. At the bottom, the braid is turned back to make a loop or eye. The lash is either leather or softened rawhide.

PLATE 23

HOW TO MAKE THE COWBOY BUTTON-KNOT

This is a knot similar to that shown in *Plate 21*, but here the weave is the "herringbone" instead of the "gaucho". It may be made any length desired and may be used for the nose-button on a bosal, as well as for many other purposes.

In the illustrations, I have used four strings to show how this knot is made. More strings may be used if desired. Just follow the same sequence as shown in the drawings.

And this brings up an important point. I have been asked on numerous occasions just how one figures out the width and number of strings required to cover a certain circumference with a woven knot.

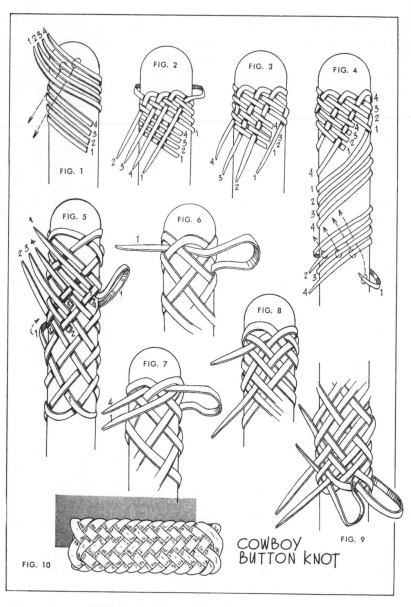

FIG. 1

FIG. 2

FIG. 3

FIG. 4

FIG. 5

FIG. 6

FIG. 7

FIG. 8

FIG. 9

FIG. 10

COWBOY
BUTTON KNOT

PLATE 23. HOW TO MAKE THE COWBOY BUTTON KNOT

Let us take this knot with four strings. When the knot is completed it will have eight bights or scallops at both top and bottom. We will consider only those at the top. A bight or scallop means that both ends of the string are used for braiding. This would give us a braid of sixteen strings. So we can apply the same simple principle to this as we do to round braids *(Plate 7)*.

Thus, if the part you want to cover with a braided knot is 2 inches in circumference and you are using a 16-string braid, this would mean that each string or thong should be ⅛ inch wide. There are sixteen ⅛ inches in 2 inches. If the core were 1 inch in circumference, you would use 1/16-inch strings.

However, where there is an over-two-under-two sequence, you have considerable leeway and do not have to figure exactly. The knot will adjust itself satisfactorily to somewhat larger or smaller circumferences.

Beginning with *Fig. 1*, the strings are spiraled around the core as shown. The standing ends may be tied down, but, as I explained in the previous Cowboy Knot *(Plate 21)*, most workers simply hold them in place with the thumb until they are covered with the braid. Better tie them down.

String No. 4 passes down over No. 3 and under No. 2. String No. 3 passes over No. 2 and under No. 1. String No. 2 will pass over No. 1 and under No. 4. String No. 1 passes around in back and over No. 4 and under No. 3. This can better be seen in *Fig. 2*.

The weave is carried down as in *Fig. 3* and then in *Fig. 4* the working ends are spiraled around the core approximately the length of the braid desired.

The same sequence is followed at the bottom as at the top. Working ends are passed upward over one and under one. *(Fig. 4)*

Braid is carried upward until the working ends join with the standing ends. It will be seen in *Fig. 5* that String No. 1 comes up alongside the RIGHT of the standing end of No. 4. String No. 4 is to the RIGHT of standing end No. 3, and so on.

Working ends pass to the top, parallel to the strings on their left. In *Fig. 6*, the working ends pass beneath the crossed strings at the top, as shown.

Follow the sequence illustrated in *Figs. 7* and *8*. At the bottom, the working ends pass over three strings and go upward again, splitting parallel pairs *(Fig. 9)*. This is continued until they come out at the beginning of the herringbone braid at the top, where they are cut off and tucked in.

The finished knot is shown in *Fig. 10*.

This knot can also be made with a Pineapple-knot braid by bringing the working end up the LEFT side of the standing part and then passing beneath the crossed strings, as shown in *Plate 11*. The Pineapple braid will close at the top and bottom and so is the best for covering the tops of quirt handles.

There are, of course, several other ways to make such knots where more than one string is used. Each oldtimer appears to have his own particular method. The end result is the same, but the manner of arriving at this end result is different. One such method consists of actually braiding on the skeleton knot and then interweaving. For instance, four strings are secured on the part to be covered. These are braided down, over one under one, in a four-string round braid. The strings are then crowned and worked upward, each alongside of its nearest string. The top strings are crowned and in working downward each splits a pair of parallel strings. This produces in the end the same knot before described.

Interesting parts of an old braided headstall, sent to the author by L. H. Rutter, Hinsdale, Montana. The keeper on the right has a loop made with an 8-string braid and then woven into a 16-string braid without core. The 16-string flattens out. This braid is illustrated under braided hobbles.

PLATE 24

HOW TO MAKE A BRAIDED LASH FOR THE ROMAL

If you wish a fancy braided *lash* for your romal take a strip of rawhide—or a piece of strap leather—24 inches long and ¾ inches wide. If rawhide is used, soften it before you start braiding.

Braid to be used is that known as the "Trick Braid", or "Inside Braid". It is a puzzle to many. On seeing it for the first time, it is hard to believe the braid can be made without its working ends being free. It is often used on belts and wrist-loops for quirts or riding crops.

Mark the middle of strip and measure off 1½ inches each way from this center. At these points slit the strip into three ¼-inch parts, cutting down on each side for about 6 inches. This is shown in *Fig. 1*.

Place the two slit parts of the strip together, the flesh sides together, as in *Fig. 2*.

In *Fig. 3*, beginning of the inside braid is shown. However, for simplicity, only one side of the rawhide strip is shown. In actual braiding, you braid both sides together at the same time.

Starting with the right-hand thong (or *thongs*, as you will be braiding two at once) marked C, place its bight over the center thong (B); then bring the bight of the left-hand thong (A) over C. It will be noticed that a reverse or compensating braid is formed at the bottom. This bottom braid must be raveled out, while the top part is to remain as it is.

To make this bottom braid disappear, pass the entire bottom end of the strip through the opening indicated in *Fig. 2*. This will twist and tangle the thongs as shown in *Fig. 4*, but do not mind this. Back part of the strip will be forward and should now be twisted from left to right until the front side is foremost. *(Fig. 5)*

After this twist, be sure that thong B is over thong A, and thong C over thong B, as shown in *Fig. 5*. Now pass the lower end up and through the opening, as shown in *Fig. 5*. Braid will appear as in *Fig. 6*. Both parts are shown here braided together.

From this point you start braiding each strip independently. First step is shown by the arrow-line in *Fig. 6*. Refer back to *Fig. 3* and continue through *Fig. 5*. Turn the work over and braid the other strip in the same fashion.

The finished lash is shown in *Fig. 7*. The ends are tapered and top part of the lash also is tapered. In working this through the loop in the end of the romal, you either make your loop after braiding on your lash, or slip it in position through the loop before you start braiding.

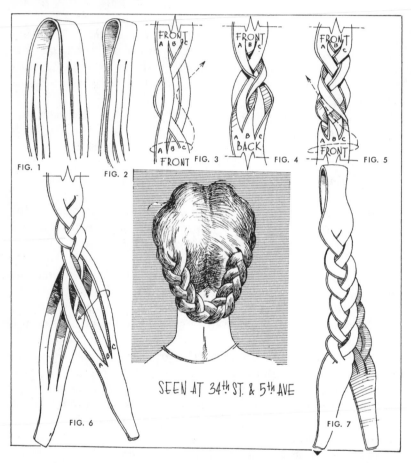

PLATE 24. HOW TO MAKE A BRAIDED LASH FOR THE ROMAL

You will notice, in looking at the romal in *Plate 22*, that a turk's head or ring-knot is worked over the upper end of the lash to make it fit snug on the loop. This is mainly for decoration, however, as the double braid in your lash will hold it on the romal loop.

In *Plate 24* is shown a curious example of feminine hairdressing. I have been able to work out many types of intricate braids, but must admit that for once I am stumped. I cannot figure this one out—but, of course, there are a lot of things about women's gear which have always been a puzzle to the male species.

PLATE 25

HOW TO MAKE A BRAIDED CURB-STRAP

One of the finest examples of the braider's art I ever came across was a beautiful rawhide "curb-strap" in the form of an excellent pen-and-ink drawing sent me by Joe De Yong, artist and writer, who had found it in Arizona. From this drawing I could see the strap as well as if I held it in my hand.

Joe De Yong, friend of the late Will Rogers, and protégé of Charles Marion Russell, the cowboy artist, had been scouting for authentic western horse gear in connection with a movie. Joe has been technical adviser for many famous western movies.

The *braided curb-strap,* shown in *Fig. 1,* is a tricky bit of gear that is completely adjustable by means of a series of woven knots.

At first glance it is hard to determine just how it is put together; but the strap is fairly simple, once you have studied it. Its simplicity makes it all the more artistic.

I made up this strap from two 15-inch lengths of 8-string braid. *(Plate 8)* The rawhide strings were 3/32 inch in width. On each end of the braid I first worked a foundation knot, as for the *San Juan honda* shown in *Plate 31.* These foundation knots were covered with small pineapple knots. *(Plate 11)*

It will be seen that the braid A terminates in an end button at the upper right and lower left. At the upper left it forms a loop. Braid B terminates in an end button at the upper left and the lower right. At the upper right it forms a loop. The two braids cross under the woven knot in the upper center.

After making your two lengths of braid, tie them together at the points where the woven knots will be. Then use whatever decorative knots you wish. I used the pineapple knot in all cases. First I placed a small ring knot *(Plate 5)* on the braid and covered this with a pineapple knot.

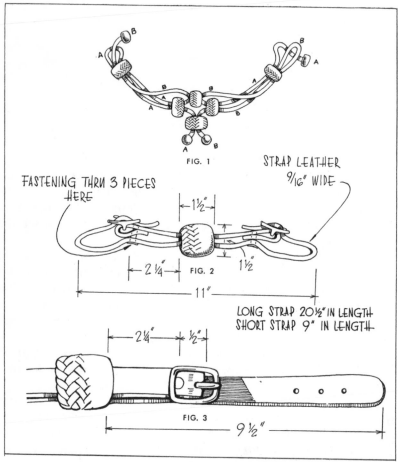

FIG. 1

STRAP LEATHER 9/16" WIDE

FASTENING THRU 3 PIECES HERE

|←1½"→|

|← 2¼"→| FIG. 2   1½"

|————— 11" —————|

LONG STRAP 20½" IN LENGTH
SHORT STRAP 9" IN LENGTH

|← 2¼" →|← ½" →|

FIG. 3

|————— 9½" —————|

PLATE 25. HOW TO MAKE A BRAIDED CURB-STRAP

This curb-strap when closed should measure about 10 inches in length. It is used, of course, with either the American or Mexican curb-bit and goes well with a braided headstall and reins.

Another type, termed a "Mexican controller bit-curb", is shown in *Figs. 2* and *3*. In the center of the strap is a rawhide braided knot which works against the tender part of the horse's chin, thus making its use highly effective. The strap is of latigo, fastened with buckles. Details and measurements are shown in *Figs. 2* and *3*.

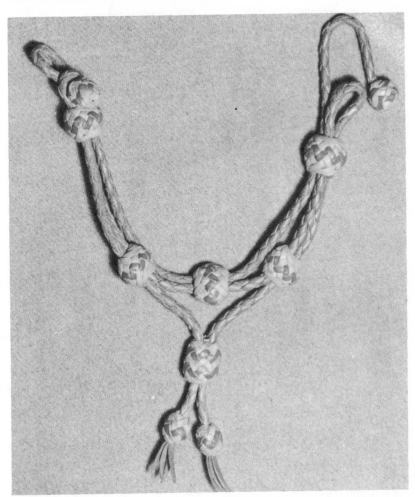

Braided rawhide curb strap made by author from design sent by Joe De Yong, Hollywood, California.

The rawhide knot is made of ¼-inch strings. It is hardened by several coats of lacquer or varnish. Several types of knots may be used, but the pineapple is the best. Make it over a foundation such as the ring knot.

PLATE 26

HOW TO MAKE A BRAIDED QUIRT

The *quirt,* or short, loaded whip, found hanging from every western saddle horn, is one of those cowboy artifacts that differ according to locality. Various sections of the West have their dif-

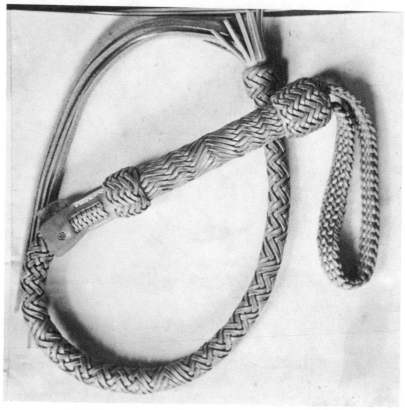

Quirt made by author with an Argentine rebenque motif.

ferent types of the whip and a close student of such matters can fairly well tell what part of the country a rider hails from by the quirt he carries.

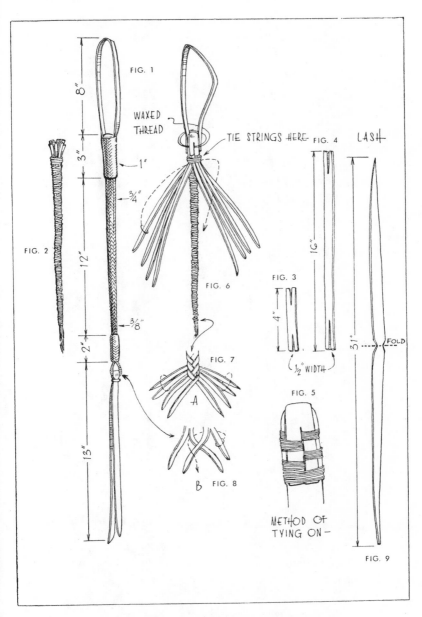

FIG. 1

FIG. 2

WAXED THREAD

TIE STRINGS HERE

FIG. 4

LASH

8"

3"

1"

3/4"

12"

3/8"

2"

15"

FIG. 6

FIG. 3

16"

4"

1/2" WIDTH

FIG. 7

A

B FIG. 8

FIG. 5

METHOD OF TYING ON—

31"

FOLD

FIG. 9

PLATE 26. HOW TO MAKE A BRAIDED QUIRT

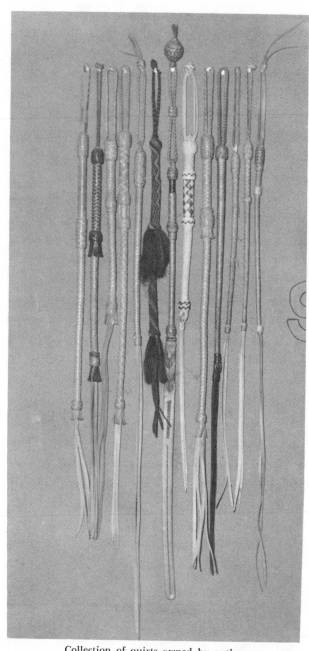

Collection of quirts owned by author.

Like other articles of cowboy gear, the quirt has its origin in Mexico, where they call it *cuarta* (kwar'-tah). Some American cowboys term it a "quisto".

A simple quirt, combining most of the best features of all types, is shown in *Fig. 1*.

The foundation, or core, is made of tapered strips of rawhide or leather, about 17 inches long, lashed together as shown in *Fig. 2*. If rawhide is used, dampen it before lashing together, roll it under foot when lashed, and then hang it up to dry, with a weight on its lower end.

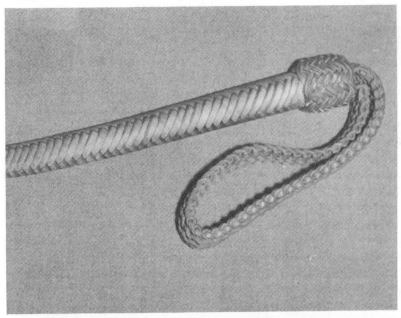

Braided quirt from Texas-Mexican border, owned by author. Knot on the handle is same type of braid as shown on Arabian knife and Argentine rebenque.

Now place over upper end of the core a small piece of rawhide or leather, such as shown in *Fig. 3*. This is lashed on as in *Fig. 5*. Next lash on the wrist-strap, which can be latigo or other type of leather, or softened rawhide. This strap is shown in *Fig. 4* and in process of being lashed on in *Fig. 5*. Both wrist-strap and covering can be lashed on at the same time, using waxed twine and passing beneath alternate ends as shown. Such a type of lashing will clinch them on tight.

Usually the flat part of the wrist-strap is at right angles to the edges of the lash at the other end. Remember this in putting on your lash.

In case you wish your quirt handle weighted, insert a short metal bar in its upper end, pushing it down into the core. You may have to cut out some middle sections of the core so that, when the metal bar is in place, the outside diameter does not swell.

Just below the ends of the wrist-loop and the covering, lash on eight rawhide strings (or leather thongs if you are working with leather). Combined width of these strings should be equal to the circumference of the core at this point. Use strings twice the length of the finished braid. They should be, in this case, about 34 inches long. Better to have too much than too little.

Braid down with the 8-string braid *(Plate 7)* until the end of the core is reached. Take a look at *Fig. 7*. Here the two upper strings on either side which are circled, are left as they are. You will not work with them any more. Take the four lower strings and make a 4-string round braid. *(Plate 30)* This is illustrated in *Fig. 8*. Braid down about 3 inches and then fold braid back to form a loop. Tuck the ends into the 8-string braid and lash them down tightly. Cut off all ends flush, including the four that were not used in the 4-string braid.

Slip your lash *(Fig. 9)* through the loop and secure it with a ring knot. *(Plate 5)* Upper and lower parts are covered with the long cowboy knot, shown in *Plate 23*.

Saddle-soap the entire quirt and, while it is damp, roll it beneath the foot to even the braid.

Perfection in rawhide braiding. A Mexican quirt owned by the author braided with 1/32-inch rawhide strings. The black interweaving is done with black horsehair.

PLATE 27

HOW TO MAKE A BRAIDED RIDING-CROP

A riding-crop usually is made over a twisted rawhide core. This core is 23 inches long and tapers from ½ inch in diameter at the handle end to ¼ inch at the other end. *(Fig. 1)* Such cores are commercially made and may be bought from whipmakers, rawhide manufacturers, and some handicraft supply stores.

The core, however, may be of rattan or elm root, or a tough flexible switch from the quince tree. Prize crops are made from the bull's pizzle, sanded down.

The first step is to lash on the wrist-strap. This may be made from a flat braid or merely a strap ⅝ inch wide. It can be tied on at the top of the handle, as shown in *Fig. 5*, or five or six inches down on the side of the core, as illustrated in *Fig. 6*. Best method of lashing on the strap is shown in *Figs. 2* and *3*. Split the strap on each end; then alternately pass the turns of waxed twine over one part and then the other, as shown in *Fig. 3*. The loop should be about 6 inches when on the crop.

Other end of the core is fitted with a short leather piece fastened on in the same manner. *(Fig. 4)* The shape of this end leather can be as you wish, either like that shown in *Fig. 4*, or those shown in *Figs. 7* and *8*.

If the wrist-loop is at the end of the handle, you can start your braid at the very top and carry it down to the smaller end, using the 8-thong braid shown in *Plate 7*, or the 12-thong as detailed in the text accompanying *Plate 8*.

If the handle end is to be braided different from the body, there are several types of braid to select from. One of these is shown in *Figs. 9, 11, 12* and *13*. This is made with a strip of leather six inches long and wide enough to encompass the core at this point. Slit the leather four times, as shown in *Fig. 9*, so that you have five strips of the same width. Lash it on at the top *(Fig. 11)* and with a different colored thong pass around over one, under one, spiraling down as illustrated in *Figs. 12* and *13*.

Same effect can be achieved with thongs, as illustrated in *Figs. 14, 15,* and *16*. In *Figs. 17* and *18* is a method of making a handle-covering with *Spanish hitching*. Other types are to be found in the book, *Leather Braiding*.

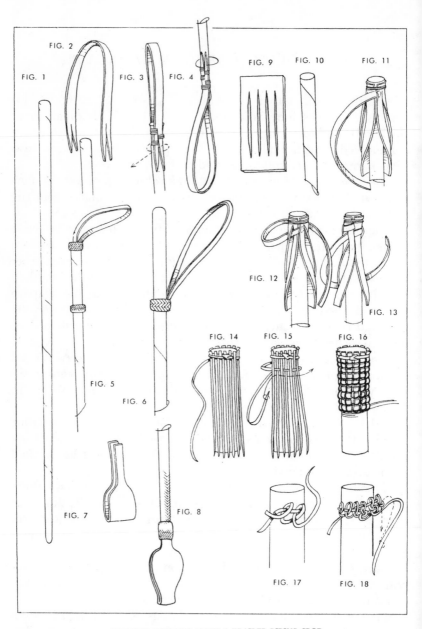

FIG. 1 FIG. 2 FIG. 3 FIG. 4 FIG. 9 FIG. 10 FIG. 11 FIG. 12 FIG. 13 FIG. 5 FIG. 6 FIG. 14 FIG. 15 FIG. 16 FIG. 7 FIG. 8 FIG. 17 FIG. 18

PLATE 27. HOW TO MAKE A BRAIDED RIDING-CROP

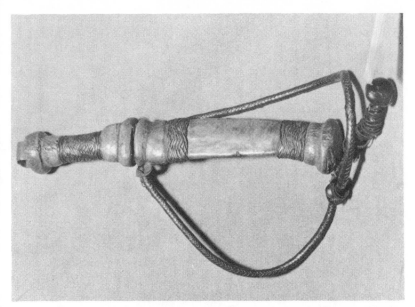

An ancient Arabian knife and sheath owned by Wright Howes, Chicago, Illinois. Note the braided knots on sheath and knife handle. Rawhide and leather braiding originated in Arabia, and was carried into Spain.

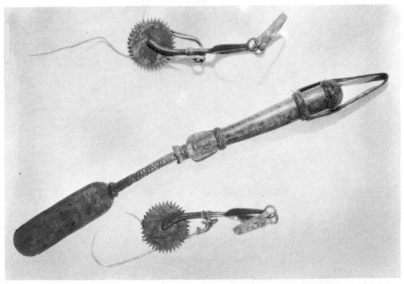

An Argentine rebenque, or heavy quirt, owned by Edward Larocque Tinker, New York, N. Y. Note braided knot on handle end of quirt, similar to that of the Arabian knife.

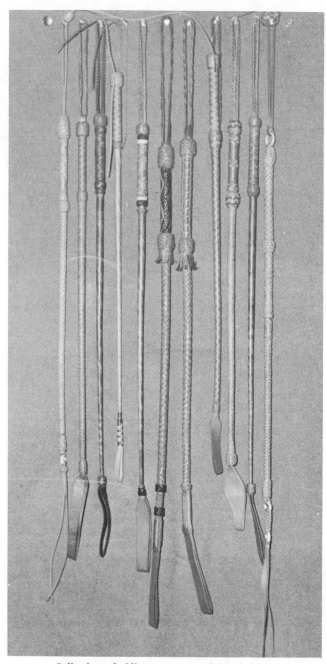

Collection of riding crops owned by author.

After the handle part is braided, the remainder of the core is covered with a braid as described above. Woven knots are used to cover all places where braids join or where ends are lashed down. (*Figs. 5, 6, and 8*) Where the wrist-strap is used on the side (*Fig. 6*), an attractive braid for the handle is shown in the next plate, 28.

PLATE 28

THE LONE STAR BRAID

I am not anxious to revive the old argument as to whether the first cowboy came from Texas or California. However, the oriflamme of the Texan, the Lone Star, is a popular decoration on cowboy gear from coast to coast. So we might say the Lone Star is the trademark of the cowboy.

This five-pointed star may of course be made with silver and other metal, or by leather carving and stamping. But it also can be worked out in braiding. I've been able to do it with a two-toned braid, as well as with a Spanish woven knot. (*Plate 37*)

The braid can be used as a handle-covering for a quirt, riding crop, romal, cane, or umbrella. The way to make it is this:

Take ten rawhide strings or leather thongs whose combined width is slightly less than the circumference of the core to be covered. Five of these strings will be white and five of a darker shade. Lash all ten strings or thongs, with the colors alternating, at the bottom of the handle to be covered, and with their flesh sides next to the core. This is shown in *Fig. 1*. Next the strings are spiraled up around the core to the top, where they are also lashed down.

Lashing at the bottom is later covered with a woven knot. However, in the case of the romal (*Plate 21*), where a finished braid is desired on the bottom, you will follow the same method as you do at the top. The way of starting this is shown in *Fig. 2*. Ends at the bottom are carried upward and join with those coming down from the top.

But to continue the sequence at the top: Bend down all the white strings, as shown in Fig. 3. With the darker ones make a crown knot. (*Figs. 3, 4, 5, and 6*) In *Fig. 7* we are looking down on this crown knot, which rests on top of the core.

Quirts and whips from all parts, in the author's collection. Left to right: Paraguayan *arreador* (cattle whip—the long one which circles the sides and tops of the others); California quirt (made by Ernie Ladouceur); Mexican quirt; South Dakota quirt (made by Burt Rogers); Texas quirt; New Mexico quirt (made by Roy Harmon); Argentine quirt; California quirt (made by Ernie Ladouceur).

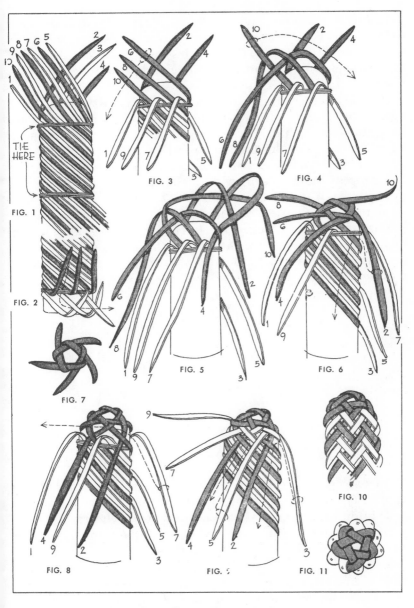

TIE HERE

FIG. 1

FIG. 2

FIG. 3

FIG. 4

FIG. 5

FIG. 6

FIG. 7

FIG. 8

FIG. 9

FIG. 10

FIG. 11

PLATE 28. THE LONE STAR BRAID

In *Fig. 6,* the down braid is started. First work with the dark strings. It will be noticed that string No. 2 passes over string No. 6 and under string No. 8. Observe this carefully. Weave the other dark strings in like manner, over one and under one, and your work will appear as in *Fig. 8.*

Next weave the white strings. In *Fig. 8,* we see that string No. 7 is brought up and over dark string No. 2; then beneath the cross formed by dark strings Nos. 8 and 4. When you have worked with all white strings in this fashion you will see that each one passes beneath three other strings—two dark and one white.

Keep your braid up snug with the star part now formed resting exactly on top of the core. You start braiding down now with all ten strings—over two and under two. The herringbone effect in this braid is shown in *Fig. 10.* In *Fig. 11,* looking down on top of the braid, you can see the *five-pointed star,* with the white strings forming the background. By working carefully, after removing the upper binding, star-knot can be closed completely at the top.

PLATE 29

HOW TO MAKE THE TAMALE

Anyone who has braided several long strings of rawhide, or another type of thong, is aware that as the work proceeds, the loose ends begin to form into a braid of their own. This reverse braid must be unraveled from time to time and the result is that the strings usually become knotted and tangled.

To avoid this, when working with long strings, braiders usually form them into what is called the *tamale.* This is a coil so fashioned that the braider can draw out from the center the quantity of string needed without destroying the shape of the tamale or causing it to collapse. By using the tamale, a lot of time and trouble are circumvented.

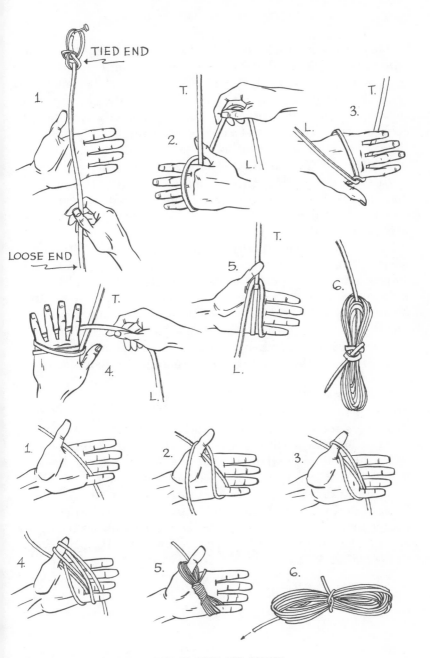

TIED END

LOOSE END

1.

2.

3.

4.

5.

6.

T.

T.

L.

L.

T.

L.

T.

L.

1.

2.

3.

4.

5.

6.

PLATE 29. HOW TO MAKE THE TAMALE

There are several ways to make this tamale. Mrs. Mary Fields, wife of Glen (Slim) Fields, of Bonanza, Oregon, has allowed me to demonstrate the method she uses in making the tamale. It might be added that building a reata is all in the day's work for the comely and energetic Mary Fiends. Not only that, but she skins her cow, cures her hide, cuts it into strings and braids everything from headstalls to reatas. A fascinating series of pictures, showing Mary Fields at work on a reata, is shown on pages 104-107.

"It takes seventy-five feet of string to make fifty feet of rope," she writes. "Don't believe it takes quite the whole seventy-five feet, but I learned a long time ago what happens if you get your string too short!"

She has had much experience with rawhide, and offers a bit of advice: "I never knew there was so much difference in hides until I made a dozen or so ropes. I had been told that the only kind of hide for a rope was a hide from some old cow that just gradually dwindled away. Well, I was frankly dubious about this until I finally got hold of one like that. I could sure tell the difference. It cut up so even and was so waxy and clear looking and braided without stretching. Now I try to get that kind of hides for all my ropes."

Now to make the tamale. Tie one end to a nail, as shown in *Fig. 1*. Bring the string down over the palm of the left hand, then, by turning the hand over and in the other direction (*Fig. 2*), the string is brought up the back of the hand. The working part of the string, held in the right hand, is then looped around the standing part, as shown in *Fig. 2*. Turn the hand again, as in *Fig. 3*, with the thumb down and double the string across the back of the hand. Continue as in *Figs. 4* and *5* until all of the string is used except enough needed to wrap it around the middle of the tamale and tie it, as shown in *Fig. 6*. The working end, the part secured to the nail at the start, will now feed out as needed.

A second method which can be used with smaller strings is shown on *Plate 29*.

PLATE 30

HOW TO BRAID A REATA OR RAWHIDE ROPE

In Mexico the *reata* (ray-ah'-tah) may be of sisal or maguey fiber, or of twisted or braided rawhide. But, in the western section of the United States, *reata* means a braided rawhide rope as distinguished from a fiber rope. It is from "la reata" that the cowboy obtained his word "lariat". Some Mexican slang concerning the *reata* is to be heard along the Border, too. To be *"muy reata"* is to be valiant, and when a man is called *"uno bueno reata"*, it means he is a gay dog with the ladies.

The *reata*—sometimes written *riata*—can be made with either a 4-string or an 8-string braid. *(Plate 7)* The 8-string is fancier and considered *muy brava,* but it is less satisfactory as a working rope. It is more for show. *Reatas* are from 40 to 85 feet in length, some even longer. They come in several diameters. The ⅜-inch is called "light"; the 7/16-inch is termed "medium"; the ½-inch is "heavy"; and the 9/16-inch is "extra heavy". These diameters are determined by the diameter of the core and thickness of the rawhide strings.

In *Fig. 1* we start braiding a 4-string *reata* over a core which is either a long rawhide string or a sash cord. Remember that the total width of the four strings should equal the circumference of the core. The strings should be ½ longer than the finished length of the *reata*—needless to say, of the best quality rawhide.

Lash the strings around the core as shown in *Fig. 1*. To start the as shown in *Fig. 2,* pass string No. 1 around to the rear and back to the front on the right, under string No. 4 and over No. 2. In *Fig. 3,* string No. 4 is carried around to the rear and to the front on the left, under string No. 3 and over string No. 1. Continue this braiding sequence to the end, keeping your braid snug and tight.

In *Fig. 5* is shown one method of finishing off the "bitter end", or the end opposite the honda. The braid is arranged as shown and a slit is made in strings Nos. 4 and 2. No. 1 passes through the slit in No. 4, and No. 3 through the slit in No. 2. *(Fig. 6)* Then two slits are made in strings Nos. 1 and 4. *(Fig. 7)* Strings Nos. 2 and 3 are passed through these slits, as shown by the arrow-line in *Fig. 7* and completed in *Fig. 8*. Or, after the step in *Fig. 6,* strings Nos. 1 and 4 and strings Nos. 3 and 2 can be slit-braided by themselves. (See *Plate 13*)

A simple honda can be made by taking a strip of rawhide $\frac{3}{4}$ inch wide and rolling it together, so that it has an inside diameter of two inches. *(Fig. 9)* After shaping it, punch a hole in the bottom, the hole to be the diameter of the *reata* braid. Pass end of the *reata* through as shown in *Fig. 9*. The four loose ends now are tied in a terminal turk's-head, as shown in *Figs. 9* and *10*. The loose ends are cut off flush with the top of the knot. *(Fig. 11)*

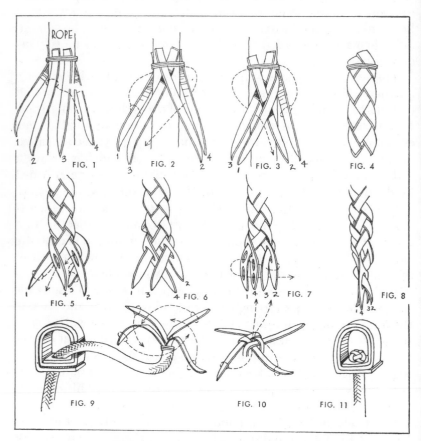

PLATE 30. HOW TO MAKE A REATA OR RAWHIDE ROPE

The *reata* should be well saddle-soaped and rolled under foot, or between two heavy boards. Some use melted tallow. It is softened by working it back and forth around a smooth post. Don't spare the elbow grease.

PLATE 31

HOW TO MAKE A SAN JUAN HONDA

The *San Juan honda* which was developed in Sonora, Mexico, is a very fancy but practical honda for the *reata*. It has a replaceable boot, or wear-leather, as will be shown.

The first step in making this honda, or eye on the working end of a *reata*, is to first middle four ¼-inch wide rawhide strings, each about 24 inches long.

When they are middled lay them one on top of the other. In *Fig. 1* it will be seen that the top string, or string No. 1, passes down through slits in strings Nos. 2, 3, and 4. Then string No. 2 passes down through slits in strings 3, 4, and 1. Next string, No. 3, passes down through strings 4, 1, and 2. In *Fig. 2,* is seen the flat side of this slit-braid; in *Fig. 3,* a three-quarters view.

A still more fancy method of making this braid is shown in *Fig. 4.* The strings are laid one on top of the other as before, but are slit-braided, so that when viewed on the edge *(Fig. 6)* they will look like a 4-string braid. In this braid, string No. 2 first passes down through a slit in string No. 3. Then string No. 3 goes up through a slit in string No. 1; No. 4 through No. 2; No. 1 through No. 4. *(Fig. 5)* Pass thus until the original top string is on the bottom and the original bottom string on top, and then begin over. The flat side of this braid is shown in *Fig. 7.*

The next step is shown in *Fig. 8.* Take a round piece of wood about ½ inch in diameter and wrap the slit-braided part around it. Now work with all eight strings, making an 8-string braid as shown in *Plate 8.* Braid down about four inches, or enough to form an inside eye of 1½ inches when the working ends are pushed up through the slit-braided eye, as shown in *Fig. 9.*

Tie together the four center strings as in *Fig. 9.* Then work the other four into a terminal knot. First *crown* the strings as shown in *Fig. 9.* Then *wall* them, or pass each string upward alternately. *(Fig. 10)* Each string now is again passed upward through the center, as shown in *Fig. 11.* All eight strings are cut off flush with the top of the knot. *(Fig. 12)*

You might find it simpler to place on your boot, or wear-leather, before pushing the braid up through the small eye and tying the terminal knot. However, the *boot* is shown in *Fig. 13.* By cutting it

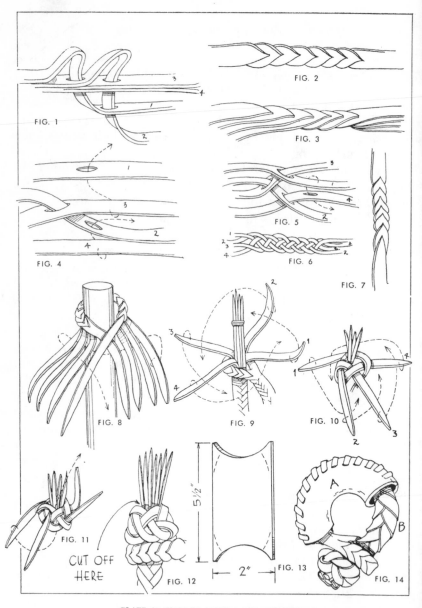

FIG. 1

FIG. 2

FIG. 3

FIG. 4

FIG. 5

FIG. 6

FIG. 7

FIG. 8

FIG. 9

FIG. 10

FIG. 11

CUT OFF HERE

FIG. 12

5½″

2″

FIG. 13

A

B

FIG. 14

PLATE 31. HOW TO MAKE A SAN JUAN HONDA

concave on its ends, the part that bends in the inner section of the eye will not buckle.

The boot is pinched together on the outside of the honda, holes are punched through both edges, and it is laced together with a rawhide string. Boot is shown in place in *Fig. 14,* designated as A. The part B is where the end of the *reata* is fastened on. *Reata* is folded around and the four working ends are tucked back into original braid. This is then covered with a woven knot, a suitable one being the *Cowboy Knot* in *Plate 21.*

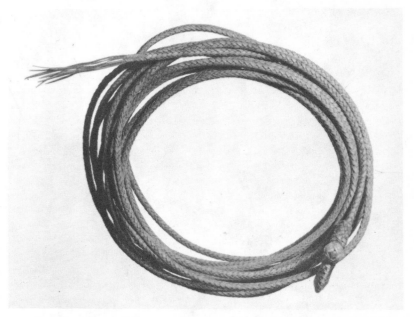

Braided rawhide reata, or lariat, with San Juan honda, made by John Conrad, Bellflower, California.

Reatas are built and not made and Mrs. Mary Fields, wife of Slim Fields of Bonanza, Oregon, is an expert, from making her own rawhide to braiding the rawhide rope.

The following series of photographs showing the various steps required to build a *reata* demonstrate the lady's ability.

1. Shaving off the hair.

2. Cutting string with a draw gauge.

3. Fleshing—splitting the rawhide string.

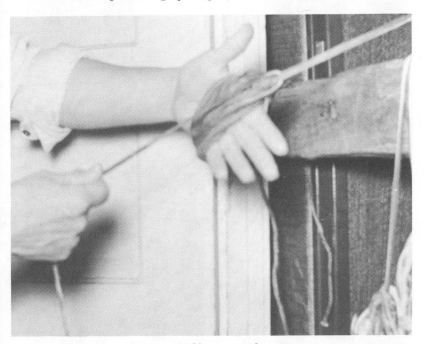

4. Making a tamale.

6. Pulling over the peg.

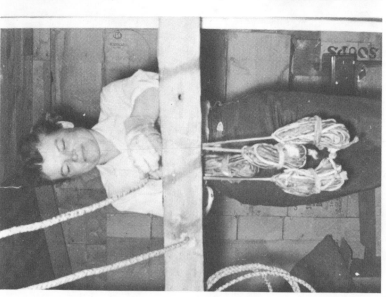

5. Braiding—the fingers are cut out of the gloves.

7. Breaking in the *reata* by pulling it through holes in a post.

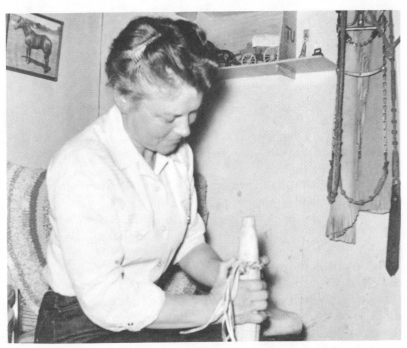

8. Shaping the honda over a stick.

PLATE 32

HOW TO TIE THE REATA TO THE HONDA

In *Plate 32* is shown one of the methods of securing the *reata* to the honda. The fastening knot is actually a five-part four-bight turk's head, but made with four strings. The same method can be used in making a longer turk's head, but the five-part turk's head is sufficient.

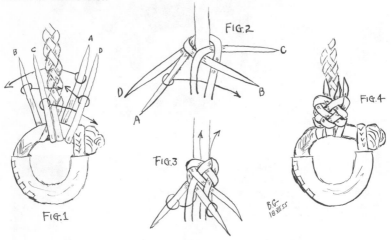

PLATE 32. HOW TO TIE THE REATA TO THE HONDA

Leave about 8 inches of the *reata* unbraided. Place it on the honda, as shown in *Fig. 1*, so that two strings come up on one side and two on the other.

The strings are now crowned about three- quarters of an inch up from the honda. Crowning means that string A is laid over string B in a counter-clockwise direction; string B then is laid over string C; string C is laid over string D, and string D is passed through the bight made in string A.

The result is shown in *Fig. 2*. Also, in this diagram it will be seen that the arrow-line indicates that string A passes over one string (C) and then under string D. In a similar manner, string B passes over string D and under string A. String C passes over string A and under string B. String D passes over string B and under string C.

The above sequence is shown in *Fig. 3*. Now each string passes over one and then completely under the knot to come out at the top. The ends, shown in *Fig. 4*, may be cut off, or they may be spliced back into the honda for several inches to give the knot more strength.

By referring to the *Short Cowboy Knot* (*Plate 21*) and the *Cowboy Button Knot* (*Plate 23*), other and fancier sequences can be worked out.

PLATE 33

THE SADDLE-HORN TIE KNOT

There is a difference in using the rawhide rope, or *reata,* and the hempen rope. The California buckaroos, who are partial to the rawhide rope, are known as "dally men." The term "dally" comes from the Mexican *dar la vuelta,* "to give a turn." In other words, the dally men turn the bitter end—or end opposite the loop —in a counter-clockwise direction several times around the horn of the saddle after throwing the rope. The rawhide rope user "dallies" his rope because a rawhide rope cannot stand the sudden strain when the cow is "busted" on the other end, and by "dallying," the rope is allowed to give or slip a trifle.

The Texan and those of his school who use the hempen or fiber rope, makes the rope fast around the saddle horn and so is termed a "tie-man." Rodeo cowboys are "tie-men," too.

There are various ways of tying a rope to the saddle horn, but Roy Harmon, of Las Cruces, picked up a practical knot for "tying" at the Socorro Rodeo and has passed it along to the author. Roy says this knot was shown him by a rodeo cowboy, Bill Rush, of Lovington, New Mexico.

"The knot is primarily used by rodeo cowboys to fix their rope to the saddle horn in such a manner that it can be easily removed," explains Roy. "It's really a slip knot. The ordinary knot used by cattlemen and working cowboys is tied in the end of the rope and, after heavy stock have been roped and dragged, the knot often tightens so that it is hard to untie. But with this one, the rope can just be slipped off the horn."

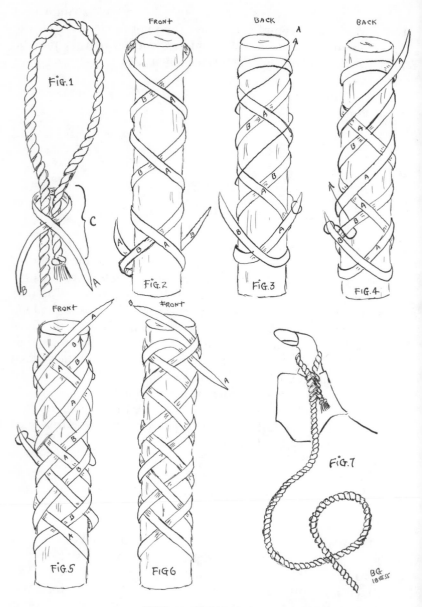

FIG.1

C

B   A

FRONT

FIG.2

A B A B A B

BACK

A

FIG.3

BACK

A

FIG.4

FRONT

A

FIG.5

FRONT

B

A

FIG.6

FIG.7

BG
18.VII.55

PLATE 33. THE SADDLE HORN TIE KNOT

To make this knot, take a string or thong of rawhide or latigo, whichever is preferred, about ⅜-inch wide and 24 inches long.

In *Fig. 1* is shown the lariat in position to receive the knot. The working area is indicated by the C. Commence the braid as shown, bringing the end of the string marked B around to the front, and then the one marked A around and over B.

In *Fig. 2,* the string-end A has passed over the string-end B three times in the front and twice in the rear. (*Fig. 3*)

It will be noticed in *Fig. 3* that when the string-end A is brought to the rear, it is then crossed under B. Now spiral A upward, crossing it over all sections of the string, as indicated by the arrow-line.

This latter step is shown in *Fig. 4*. Also, the arrow-line in Fig. *4* indicates how B passes beneath its own part. The arrow-line in *Fig. 5* indicates how B is worked upward, interlocking the braid.

The finished braid is shown in *Fig. 6*. The saddle-horn knot is shown in place in *Fig. 7*.

This knot can be made any length and can be used for bosal nose buttons and other coverings. It may, of course, be interwoven with the gaucho or herringbone braid.

PLATE 34

HOW TO MAKE SIMPLE TYPES OF HOBBLES

Hobbles come in many styles. They vary from the simplest form, such as is made from a torn gunny sack and piece of rope, to the more elaborately braided article.

Attractive and workable hobbles may be fashioned from ordinary strap leather (or softened rawhide, if you like) of about ⅛ inch in thickness.

The over-all length of the strap is 29 inches and it is 3 inches wide. Taper it from each end for 12 inches, so that the center portion is 2 inches wide. *(Fig. 1)* Round off the ends and punch a hole an inch from each end, in the center of the strap. Make a slit 2½ inches long from each of these holes toward the center, or middle portion, of the strap. These slits serve as holes to accommodate the button.

One method of making the button and securing it to the strap is shown in *Fig. 1*. This is by a three-hole fastening. Holes are punched as shown, each set of three holes being about 3 inches from the middle of the strap. Thus they would be 6 inches apart.

Thread a ¼-inch thong through the holes as illustrated and then split the ends. Tie these ends in a *terminal turk's-head* knot, as explained in *Plate 30*, or the *end knot* shown in *Plate 31*.

In *Fig. 2*, another method is demonstrated for making the button and securing it with only one hole punched on each side.

Also, the *rolled leather button* may be used with three holes, as shown in *Figs. 3, 4,* and *5*.

In *Fig. 6* a metal ring 1½ inches inside diameter is used in the center of the hobble shown. The ends of the strap are folded over the ring, secured with a Spanish ring-knot *(Plate 5)* and the ends are slit and worked into a terminal knot. This terminal knot can be covered with a woven knot, such as the pineapple. *(Plate 11)*

A slit-braid hobble that I worked out, and which has proved a practical one, is illustrated in *Fig. 7*. It is made of two pieces of leather each 26 inches long. These are tapered down from 3 inches in width at the button-end to 1-inch width at 12 inches from that end. (The taper is not plainly shown in the drawings.)

The two inside ends are joined together by a slit-braid. Strap A is placed over strap B and two slits are made, one in strap A and one in strap B, as shown in *Fig. 8*. Slit in B should be 12 inches from the button-end of the strap. The one in A should be 13 inches from the button-end.

Strap A is pushed down through B and then B up through A, indicated by arrow-lines in *Fig. 8*. A final slit is made in B, and A is pushed up through this. *(Fig. 9)*

The leather should be damp in working this slit-braid.

In *Fig. 10,* it is seen that both the ends A and B have been slit into four thongs. These thongs are worked into terminal turk's-heads and then covered with a woven knot (pineapple knot, *Plate 11*), if desired.

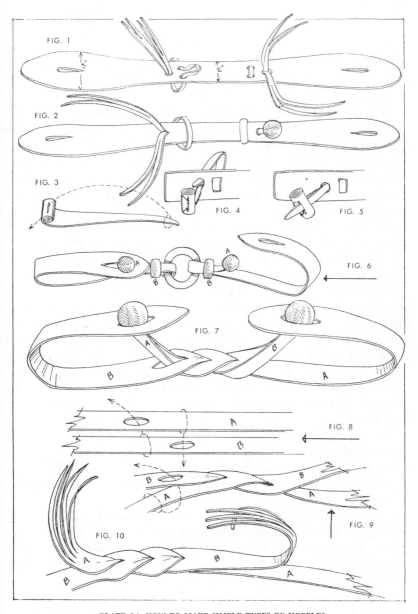

FIG. 1

FIG. 2

FIG. 3

FIG. 4

FIG. 5

FIG. 6

FIG. 7

FIG. 8

FIG. 9

FIG. 10

PLATE 34. HOW TO MAKE SIMPLE TYPES OF HOBBLES

PLATE 35

HOW TO MAKE A PAIR OF BRAIDED GAUCHO HOBBLES

These hobbles are made in the most tricky fashion of any I've ever seen. They were brought back from the Argentine by Edward Larocque Tinker, who acquired them while writing his book, *Los Jinetes de las Americas y la Literatura Por Ellos Inspirada* (Horsemen of the Americas and Literature They Inspired). Tinker loaned me the hobbles with the suggestion that I "figure this one out".

At first glance it appears almost impossible that the inside 8-string braid could have been made in the middle section of the hobbles. However, a closer study shows they are fashioned in two parts, ending in buttons A and B *(Fig. 1)*.

First take two pieces of leather (or softened rawhide, as used for the originals) each 26 inches long and 3 inches wide. Mark off 12 inches from one end and taper this down to 2 inches wide, tapering on both edges, of course. The remainder of 14 inches should be 2 inches in width, and this is split into eight ¼-inch thongs. Then, as in *Fig. 2*, cut out every other thong, leaving only four thongs. (This also is done for the other piece, marked A in *Fig. 5*. It will be noticed that you start cutting out the thongs from opposite side on A).

Take a small round stick, about ⅜ inch in diameter, for use as a mandrel, as shown in *Fig. 3*.

Begin a 4-thong braid *(Plate 30)* for some 3 inches. As this braid must be interwoven by the thongs on the other piece of leather, make it loose. *(Fig. 4)*

In *Fig. 5* you marry or join the other thongs of A. To do this, thong No. 5 passes along the upper side of thong No. 2; No. 6 along the upper side of No. 1. Continue doubling these thongs toward the left, until they come out on the inside of the leather piece marked B. *(Fig. 6)*

In *Fig. 6* you begin to interweave. You will note that the remaining, or lower thongs of A, split pairs as shown. The sequence is over two under two, until thongs are also on the left inside of leather piece B.

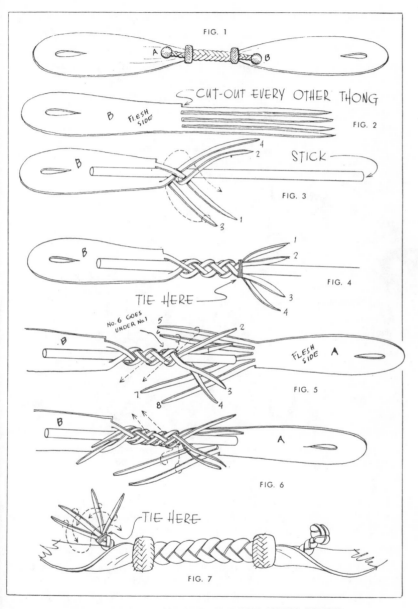

FIG. 1

CUT-OUT EVERY OTHER THONG

B FLESH SIDE

FIG. 2

B

STICK

FIG. 3

4
2
1
3

B

1
2
3
4

TIE HERE

FIG. 4

No. 6 GOES UNDER No. 1

B

5
2

FLESH SIDE A

7
8
3
4

FIG. 5

B

A

FIG. 6

TIE HERE

FIG. 7

PLATE 35. HOW TO MAKE A PAIR OF BRAIDED GAUCHO HOBBLES

Remove the mandrel and tighten your braid. The four thongs on either end are braided for an inch or so in a four-thong round braid *(Plate 30)* and then tied in a terminal turk's-head, as indicated by the arrow-lines in *Fig. 7*. For this turk's-head, see *Plate 30*, or you might wish to use the one in *Plate 31*.

Cover both ends of the 8-thong braid with a pineapple knot *(Plate 11)* and also work a similar knot over the terminal turk's-heads.

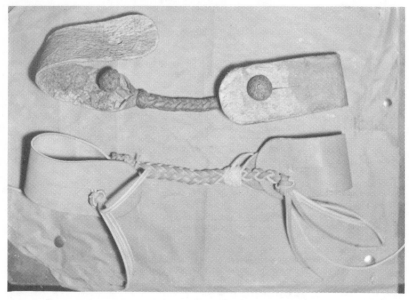

Gaucho hobbles *(upper)* owned by Edward Larocque Tinker, New York, N. Y. Duplicate *(lower)* made by author to illustrate the trick method of making these hobbles.

There are other ways of making this inside braid of eight thongs, but I have found the above method the simplest and least confusing. However, if you like, you may first braid the eight thongs on the part B into an 8-thong braid *(Plate 8)*—that is, before cutting out four thongs as previously described. But the four that would have been cut out should be clearly marked. These are then replaced by four thongs on the part A. As replacement progresses, draw back the marked thongs and finally, when all thongs on the A end have been interwoven, cut off excess strings on B. This produces the same result as before.

PLATE 36

HOW TO MAKE A PAIR OF BRAIDED HOBBLES

These are made entirely of braidwork and have the *Lone Star* design woven in the buttons.

The first step in making these fancy hobbles is to cover a metal ring, 1½ inch in diameter, with rawhide braiding as described in *Plate 14.* This covered ring is indicated as A in *Fig. 1.*

Braided rawhide hobbles made by John Conrad, Bellflower, California.

The cuffs, B and C in *Fig. 1,* are made as follows:

Take eight ⅛-inch rawhide strings, each 56 inches long. Middle them and from this point measure off four inches. Start an 8-string braid *(Plate 8)* here, working back toward the middle of the strings and beyond until you have six inches of the braid. This will form the loop for your button.

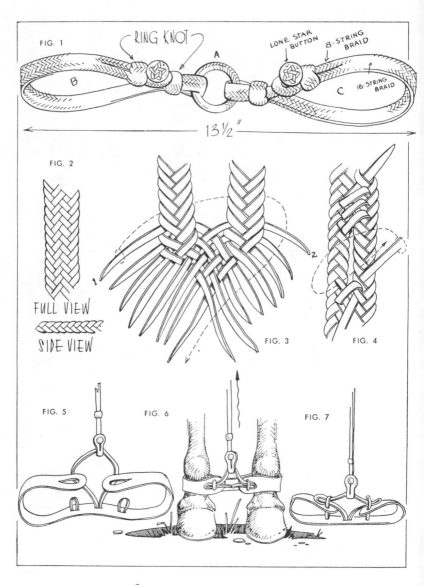

FIG. 1

RING KNOT

A

LONE STAR BUTTON

8-STRING BRAID

B

C

16-STRING BRAID

13½"

FIG. 2

FULL VIEW

SIDE VIEW

FIG. 3

FIG. 4

FIG. 5

FIG. 6

FIG. 7

PLATE 36. HOW TO MAKE A PAIR OF BRAIDED HOBBLES

Now bring the strings from each end of the braid together. There will be sixteen of them. Arrange them as shown in *Fig. 3*. Interweave the strings as shown and then begin your braid by first bringing the highest string on the left (No. 1) around to the rear and forward on the right under two, over two, under two, and over two. Next string No. 2 on the right passes around to the back and forward under two, over two, under two, and over two.

This 16-string braid is continued for 15 inches. As it is made without a core, it should be pressed flat from the top when finished. It then will appear as a double flat braid and the front part will look like the top drawing and the edges like the lower drawing in *Fig. 2*.

When the 16-string braid is finished, tie it together at the end. Now, with the loose strings make a terminal knot. This can be done by taking four outside strings and working them into a terminal turk's-head *(Plate 30)* around the other twelve. Cover this turk's-head with the Lone Star Knot. *(Plate 37)*

Two keeper-knots are necessary on each side, one to hold the cuff part of the hobbles to the ring, the other to close the loop around the button. These can be any woven knot you wish,—the Spanish Ring Knot *(Plate 5)* is a practical one.

Should you care to make your hobbles with the 8-string braid throughout by doubling it, the two braids can be held together by lacing in a long string, as shown in *Fig. 4*. At the bottom of this drawing is shown the method of starting and at the top is shown some of the finished braid. It will be noticed that the V's on the left of the braid point up, while those on the right point down.

Both this 16-string braid flattened out, and the 8-string ones laced together are good braids to be used on other articles, such as nose-bands, brow-bands, and cheek-pieces on headstalls.

At the bottom of *Plate 36* in *Figs. 5, 6,* and *7* is a unique type of hobble used in the Argentine which enables a rider to restrain his horse until he releases the hobbles when in the saddle. These are used when he has no companion to hold the fractious animal. Such hobbles are called *manea desprendedora,* which might be trans-lated as "let-loose hobbles".

PLATE 37

HOW TO MAKE THE LONE STAR KNOT

The Texas *Lone Star Knot* is a decorative button knot or a finishing knot on the end of a piece of braid or a quirt handle. It is an appropriate one for the button knot on the hobbles in *Plate 36*.

For clarification the knot here is shown made on a mandrel having a leather collar. The mandrel is divided into four areas, or sections, numbered clockwise from 1 to 4, section 1 being the front and that marked 3 the back.

The foundation knot is a 6-part, 5-bight turk's head. Its five bights or scallops provide the design for the *five-pointed star*.

Start as in *Fig. 1*. Pass the working end of the rawhide string or leather thong around the top of the mandrel and then down on the right side and over the standing part as shown.

In *Fig. 2* you are looking at the back part of the mandrel. Here the working end passes beneath the bight at the top.

Now bring your working end to the front, as in *Fig. 3*, and beneath the standing part and over the part on the left. In *Fig. 4* we are again at the back. Sequence is over one and under one.

Fig. 5—Pass down over one, under one, over one.

Fig. 6—Pass up under one, over one, under one.

Fig. 7—Down under one, over one, under one, over one.

Fig. 8—Up over one, under one, over one, under one.

Fig. 9—Down over one, under one, over one, under one, over one.

Fig. 10—When you pass under one to the left of the standing part, the skeleton or foundation knot is complete. While in these drawings we continue with the same string, showing it in a different tone, to obtain the star effect in interweaving it is necessary to begin at this point with a different colored string. The sequence will be under one, over one, under one, over one, following along to the left of the standing part.

It might be pointed out that the weave here is the same as that of the pineapple knot *(Plate 11)* at the top; at the bottom it differs in that the bight is formed on the outside of the knot instead of inside.

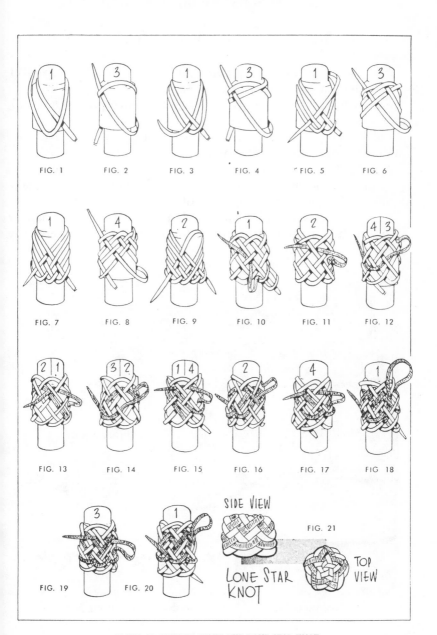

FIG. 1   FIG. 2   FIG. 3   FIG. 4   FIG. 5   FIG. 6

FIG. 7   FIG. 8   FIG. 9   FIG. 10   FIG. 11   FIG. 12

FIG. 13   FIG. 14   FIG. 15   FIG. 16   FIG. 17   FIG 18

FIG. 19   FIG. 20

SIDE VIEW

FIG. 21

LONE STAR KNOT

TOP VIEW

PLATE 37. HOW TO MAKE THE LONE STAR KNOT

Fig. 11—Under two. *Fig. 12*—Over one, under one, over two, under one.

Fig. 13—Over one, under two (splitting a pair). *Fig. 14*—Over two, under one, over two (crossed strings), under two.

Fig. 15—Over one, under two (crossed strings). *Fig. 16*—Over two, under two, over two (crossed strings), under two.

Fig. 17—Over two, under two (crossed strings). *Fig. 18*—Over two, under two, over three, under two.

Fig. 19—Over two, under three. *Fig. 20*—Over two, under two, over three. Working end is now passed under one (or two to make it more secure) at the starting point of the interweave.

Knot is removed from the mandrel and placed in its permanent position. It is tightened until the top closes. Side view and top view are shown in *Fig. 21*.

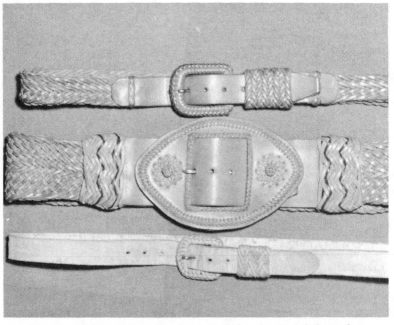

Fancy braided rawhide and leather belts designed and made by author.

PLATE 38

EIGHT-STRING ROUND EDGE BRAIDING

The name is confusing. The edge braid actually is made with one long string, but, when the braid is finished, it looks like an eight-string round braid, with a sequence of over one, under one.

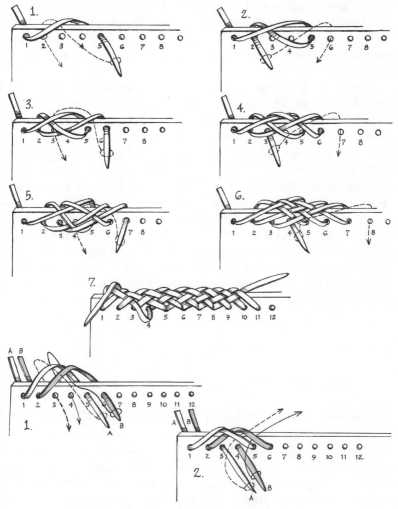

PLATE 38. EIGHT-STRING ROUND EDGE BRAIDING

This is a practical braid for securing the lining to the skirting of a saddle and, with wider thongs, is sometimes used on the cantle of the saddle. Such saddle decorations are not seen nowadays. This is too bad, for a saddle could really be dressed up and beautified with numerous types of braids and fancy knots—and in earlier times they actually were. This is another phase in the lost art of braiding. A book could be written on this subject.

This edge braid is primarily used to join two pieces together, as well as to cover and decorate the raw edges. In our diagram, for simplicity's sake, we have shown it worked on the edge of one piece of leather.

The rawhide string or leather thong, whichever you prefer, is passed through hole No. 1 from the rear and over the edge through hole No 5, also fom the rear The arrow-line shows the course of the string or thong, passing under its own part on top and then through hole No. 2 from the back. The sequence from then on is clearly illustrated in the diagrams. To finish off the starting point, the original end is worked forward and back, as shown in *Fig. 7*. To completely finish the braid at this end, the string will have to pass through hole No. 1 at least two more times.

At the bottom of *Plate 38,* two sequences are shown where two strings, or thongs, of contrasting color are worked simultaneously. The sequence given is the beginning of an under two, over two braid, which is explained more fully in the next plate, although of but one string. This edge braid gives a very pretty effect.

PLATE 39

EIGHT-STRING ROUND EDGE BRAIDING

This edge braid and similar ones which can be made by this method, are, as far as the author knows, his own invention. Sooner or later in braiding, as in many other arts and crafts, the "original" turns out to be something someone else thought of years ago. Such may happen in this case, as the working out of this braid seems to come as a natural sequence to the one shown in *Plate 38.*

This is a braid which can be made with an over two, under two sequence, and, by leaving a greater number of holes vacant on the

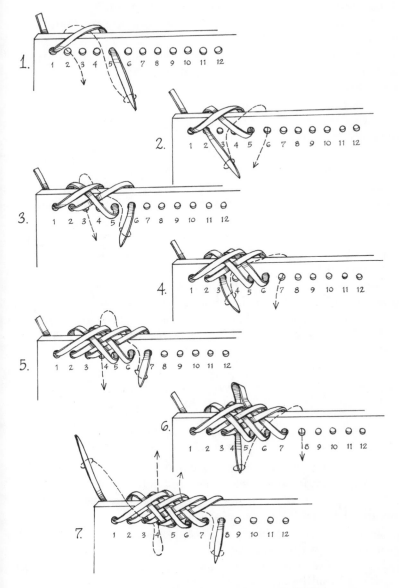

PLATE 39. EIGHT-STRING ROUND EDGE BRAIDING

first pass, can be made into a braid of over three, under three, and so on. In other words, it can be made to simulate an eight-string round braid of over two, under two, or a twelve-string round braid of over three, under three, and so on. Many combinations can be worked out.

It is a decorative edge braid and when finished looks, as one fellow remarked, "as if it just growed there."

The first and second moves, shown in *Figs. 1* and *2*, are similar to the start of the braid in *Plate 38*. But it will be noticed in *Fig. 3* that the thong or string, after passing to the front through hole No. 6, then goes under two. In *Fig. 4* it also passes under two in *Fig. 5*, it passes under two and then over one in the rear before coming to the front through hole No. 4. In *Fig. 6*, the string passes over one, under two and comes out through hole No. 8. It passes to the back, then *(Fig. 7)* under two, over one and forward through hole No. 5.

The continued sequence is, in front, always over one, under two; in the rear, under two, over one. By backbraiding at the start, you can finish off this section.

Should you care for a simulated twelve-string round braid, skip six holes at the start and the final sequence will be, at the front, over two, under three, and at the back, under three and over two.

Worked on a saddle, this makes a beautiful—and practical—decoration.

PLATE 40

SADDLE DECORATION—APPLIQUE BRAIDS

Fortunately, there are many horsemen who still consider leather carving and braidwork the richest and most agreeable form of decoration for all types of horse gear. That this form of decoration can be applied to saddles is to be seen in many old-time saddlers' catalogues, where fancy braidwork is emphasized. Unfortunately, braiding on saddles has been supplanted today by ornate and heavy metal ornaments. Only fancy carving has survived and braiding, as a saddle decoration, has become a lost art.

There are many types of braid which may be applied to saddle decoration. In an endeavor to revive this interesting and beautiful type of ornamentation, several original braids have been

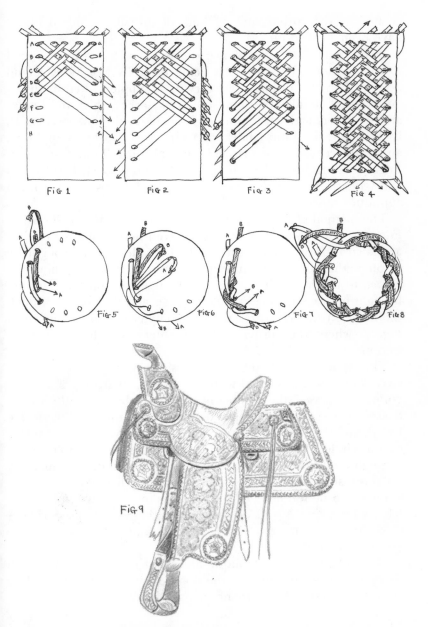

Fig 1   Fig 2   Fig 3   Fig 4

Fig 5   Fig 6   Fig 7   Fig 8

Fig 9

PLATE 40. SADDLE DECORATION APPLIQUE BRAIDS

created by the author, and methods of utilizing standard braids have been worked out.

In *Fig. 9* of *Plate 40* is shown the sketch of a saddle decorated in this fashion. This saddle is being made by Lee M. Rice and decorated by the author. The carving is supplemented by different types of braidwork. The seat, back jockey, skirt and fender are decorated with an appliqué of five strings. The swell, seat, back jockey, skirt and fender carry circles of hair-braid appliqué, and in the center of each circle is an appliquéd "Lone Star" knot. Edge braiding is on the cantle, swell, rigging, skirt, back jockey and fender. Around the horn and on the stirrups is a hair-braid appliqué.

The method of making the appliqué of five strings is shown in *Figs. 1 - 4*, inclusive. The five strings are inserted in holes or slits, as shown in *Fig. 1*. Each end on the left side is then brought up through the hole above it and then passed down, as shown in *Fig. 2*, to the holes on the right. The five ends on the right are brought up, each through the hole above, and then down through the holes on the left (*Fig. 3*). The completed braid is shown in *Fig. 4*, where the corner ends are interwoven to finish these sections.

The circle of hair-braid appliqué is shown in *Figs. 5 - 8*, inclusive. This braid is worked with two strings. If strings of a different color are used, the number of holes must be even, otherwise it doesn't matter. String B passes down through the first hole to the fourth and then back up through the hole above it, on the inside of the circle. String A passes through the second hole, down through the fifth and up through the hole above it, also emerging on the inside of the circle. (*Fig. 5*) In *Fig 6* is the key to the sequence to be followed. String B passes over its own part to the left under string A and down through the sixth hole. String A goes over its own part under string B and down through the seventh hole and so on.

Many other types of appliqué braid which can be used in such decoration will be found in the book, *Leather Braiding*. White rawhide strings or latigo thongs may be used.

PLATE 41

LONE STAR KNOT APPLIQUE

To make the "Lone Star" knot appliqué, first make the foundation or skeleton knot, as shown in *Plate 37* up to and including
Fig. 10. Do not start interweaving, as shown in *Fig. 10* of this
plate, but begin the interweave as shown in *Fig. 1, Plate 41.*

Before this, however, the foundation knot is flattened out. The
top of the knot becomes the center and the bottom of the knot
becomes the edges. Lay this flattened knot in the center of your
hair-braid appliqué circle. Then punch five holes, as shown in
Fig. 1, Plate 41. These holes are numbered 1 to 5.

Begin the weave by passing the darker colored string, designated
as B, up through hole No. 1. The string then follows the course
shown by the arrow-line in *Fig. 1.* This is under one, passing also
under, or at the tip of, string A, over one, under one, over one,
under two, over one, under one, over one, under one, and then
down through hole No. 1, passing over its own part in going
through this hole.

In *Fig. 2,* the first step of the weave is completed. String B now
follows the course of the arrow-line: down through hole No. 1,
as previously stated, up through hole No. 2, under one, over one,
under one, over one, under three, splitting a pair, over one, under
one, over one, under two, splitting a pair.

Fig. 3 shows this second phase of the braid completed. String
B now follows the course of the arrow-line, which is down through
hole No. 2, up through hole No. 3, under one, over one, under
one, splitting a pair, over two, under three, splitting a pair, over
one, under one, over two, under two.

In *Fig. 4,* the third phase of the braid is completed. The string
now follows the arrow-line: down through hole No. 3, up through
hole No. 4, under one, over one, under two, over two, under three,
over one, under two, over two, under two.

The fourth phase of the braid is completed in *Fig. 5.* String B
follows the course of the arrow-line: down through hole No. 4, up
through hole No. 5, under one, over two, under two, over two,
under three, over two, under two, over two, under two. It passes
down through hole No. 5.

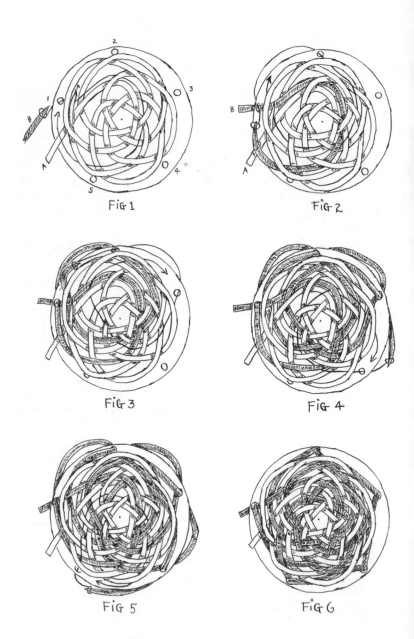

Fig 1

Fig 2

Fig 3

Fig 4

Fig 5

Fig 6

PLATE 41. LONE STAR KNOT APPLIQUE

The finished braid is shown in *Fig. 6*. The interweaving, whereby string B has passed through five holes, has secured the entire knot to the saddle leather.

Conchas for the tie strings may be fashioned from a circle of leather with edge braiding, or it may be made from a flattened "Lone Star" knot *(Plate 37)* with a smaller piece of round leather laid on top.

NOTES

Ernie Ladouceur of Madera, California, has a method of sizing sleazy leather which stiffens and glazes it and also makes it water-proof. However, a word of caution. As *white gasoline* is used in this process, great care must be exercised and it is advisable to do your work out-of-doors.

"I take a quart of white gasoline—the ordinary automobile fuel will not do—and set it in the hot sun to warm good, or in a pail of hot water," Ernie writes.

"I use a quart fruit jar with the lid put on loose. I don't screw it down tight, as vapor pressure may build up and break the glass. I work out-of-doors away from any fire or flame. When the gasoline is warm, I take some Parawax, the kind a woman uses to seal a jar of jelly with, and shave this up with a knife and put in all that the gasoline will dissolve. If there is too much wax, this won't do any harm.

"When the wax is all dissolved, I put in my leather thongs and let them stand in the solution for a couple of hours. After this, I hang them in a sunny, windy place away from any chance of catching fire, and let them dry.

"You will be surprised at what this wax filling will do to a piece of leather. If you treat your leather before you bevel it, you will be delighted at the ease with which it cuts. You will like the feel of it and how it looks after braiding.

"But be very careful. The fumes from white gasoline travel a great distance and *will ignite from a flame fifty feet away*. These fumes are heavy and flow along the ground or floor."

There are various ways to dye rawhide strings. The ordinary vegetable dyes on the market are good, especially the so-called Easter egg dyes. However, the dye solution should be only luke-warm, not hot, when the rawhide is placed in it.

John Conrad once wrote me that he had perfected a method whereby he could keep the rawhide the same color as the animal's hair. An animal with white hair produced white rawhide and, while he was in business, his pure white rawhide was of the very best. Conrad never explained his method.

To obtain black rawhide, the gauchos of the Argentine take the residue of their native drink, *yerba mate* (sometimes called Para-guayan tea), and place it in water with rusty iron. This produces a jet black liquid in which the rawhide is soaked for several days. The rawhide comes out a bluish black which is indelible. It is dyed throughout, not just on the surface.

This same result can be obtained with a strong solution of tea and rusty iron. Strain off the liquid and soak the rawhide in it for a couple of days. This produces a kind of gunmetal black.

*   *   *   *

Much fine braiding is done in South America with dried intes-tines, or what we term catgut. To make catgut, steep the intestine of any animal in water for a day, peel off the outer membrane, then turn the gut inside out, which is easily done by turning a very short piece of it inside out, just as you would turn up the cuff of your sleeve; then, catching hold of the turned up cuff, dip the whole in a bucket, and scoop up a little water between the cuff and the rest of the gut. The weight of this water will do what is wanted. It will bear down an additional length of the previously turned gut, and thus, by a few successive dippings, the entire length of any amount of intestine, however narrow it may be, can be turned inside out in a minute or two. Having turned the intestine inside out, scrape off the whole of its inner soft parts and that which remains is a fine transparent tube. This, being twisted and stretched to dry, forms catgut.

*   *   *   *

A fine sewing thread can be made from the outer membrane of intestines. Steep the intestines of any animal in water for a day. Then peel off the outer membrane, which will come off in long

strips. These should be twisted between the hands, and hung out
to dry. This thread is excellent for sewing rawhide together or
for any other purpose.

*   *   *   *

With the exception of nylon, I know of nothing tougher than
sinew. Nylon is difficult to work with, as it stretches. But sinew
will not stretch. Any sinews will do for making thread if the
fibers will submit to being twisted or braided together into pieces
of sufficient length. The sinews lying alongside the backbone of
cattle are the most convenient, on account of the length of their
fibers. After the sinew is dried, straight strips are torn off of it of
the proper size. These strips are wetted and scraped into evenness
by being drawn through the mouth and teeth. Then, by one or
two rubs between the hand and thigh, they become twisted and
their fibers are held together. A piece of dried sinew is usually
kept in reserve for making thread or string. Nothing can compare
with it.

Nothing is as good as saddle soap for preserving leather and
rawhide. All horse gear should be periodically cleaned with saddle soap—and cleaned and cleaned and cleaned. The very best
dressing for leather is made from one part lanolin and one part
neat's-foot oil. *Neat* are cattle of the ox-kind and neat's—foot is
an ox's foot. You can make your own neat's-foot oil by boiling the
feet and shin bones of neat cattle. Lanolin is wool fat.

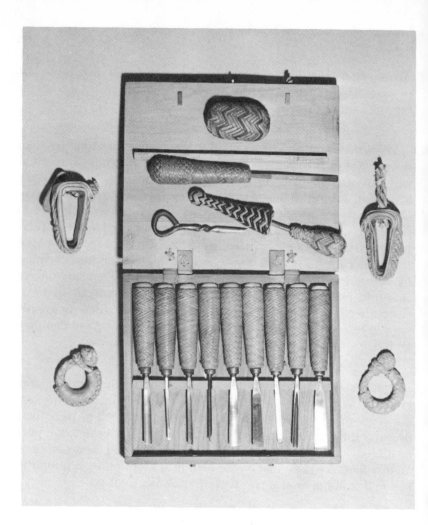

Braid Miscellanea. The box contains a set of wood carving tools, the handles of which are covered with a variety of braided knots made by the author. On the lid at the top is a rock, covered with rawhide braiding, used as a paperweight. Below is a chisel with a braid-covered handle and below this a fid and case—all braidwork by the author. To the left of the fid is a practical metal fid made by Mrs. Mary Fields. To the left of the box at the top is a honda made by Burt Rogers. Below is a honda made by John Conrad. To the right at the top is another honda made by Burt Rogers with a portion of a twisted rawhide *reata*. Below this is a honda made by the author with a braided boot.

Jesse Wilkinson of Paso Robles, California, standing beside an exhibit of some of his beautiful braidwork. Jesse is among the last of the great braiders. He was 72 when this picture was taken and had been doing rawhide braiding for some sixty years. "I can still do it fairly well," he writes modestly. Photograph by Stevens Studios, Paso Robles.

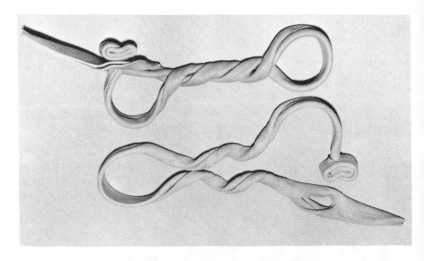

Twisted hobbles. The upper, closed pair were made by the author. The lower, open pair were made by Rudy Mudra, Sheridan, Wyoming. Both are made of heavy latigo, but can be fashioned from softened rawhide. First take a strip of latigo or rawhide 56 inches long and 2¾ inches wide. Wet thoroughly and then fold in the flesh side on both edges. On one end fashion a rolled leather button similar to the one in *Fig. 3, Plate 34*. Five and one-half inches from the button fold the leather again for 8 inches, leave 9 inches doubled after that and then fold again for 8 inches. Twist your two ⅛-inch folds together and lash with string until dry. Make a slit in the end opposite from the button. Button the hobbles and allow them to dry in the shape shown in the upper photograph. Those shown were dried around two soup cans, but they can be dried around anything approximately 3 inches in diameter. When dry, remove the string around the twisted parts. These hobbles will then retain their shape.

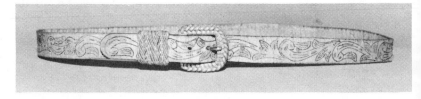

Carved rawhide belt, made by the author. This type of work offers fine possibilities. The design is carved and the cuts filled with India Ink. Work is then waxed or lacquered.

A curiosity in braiding. This is an eight-string round braid worked into a ring like a turk's head, and done with one long string, according to the maker, Ernie Ladouceur. He writes: "All I can remember was that I took a piece of copper wire and bent it in a circle. The wire was about ⅛-inch in diameter. I started working over this wire and when the braid started to get too tight I just pulled out the wire and continued from there. I haven't the slightest idea how I did it."

However, this braid can be made with *two* strings, wrapping them in the same direction, but so as to cross each other, and interweaving them. The braid is of two cycles, which would make it theoretically impossible with one string revolving in one cycle. But Ernie apparently did the impossible, which should confound all mathematicians.

This braid is certainly a challenge to the braider. It is suggested that the work first be done over a rope grommet or a metal ring. Spiral one string or thong around the grommet in a clockwise direction. Then, going in the same direction, spiral the second string around in a counter-clockwise direction so that it crosses the first string on the outside and inside of the grommet. Then wrap the first string around, passing over everything. Finally, work with the second string, over one, under one, interlocking all sections. This gives a four-string round turk's head.

This can be built into an eight-string by doubling and then splitting pairs, and after that it can be made into a sixteen-string round turk's head, and so on *ad infinitum*. If you can make this of rawhide you can do away with metal rings on your horse gear.

GLOSSARY

ALFORJA *(al-for'hah)*. Wide leather or canvas bag in which a horseman carries his personal effects on a pack animal.

APAREJO *(ah-par-ay'ho)*. Packsaddle.

BIT. The metal part of a bridle which goes in the "bit hole" of a horse's mouth and to which the reins and headstall are attached.

BIT-CHAINS. Chains for fastening the reins to the bit. Usually fitted because of the tendency of some horses to bite the reins. Also to add weight when certain types of bits, such as the Mexican, are used.

BOOTS. Protective coverings of rawhide or leather in eyes of hondas, reins, and bit-cheek loops on headstalls to prevent wear on the braid. Also called *wear-leathers*.

BOSAL *(boh-zal)*. Noseband of the hackamore, usually made of braided rawhide. Bosals are made from pencil size to a 1¼-inch diameter.

BREAST-COLLAR. Harness which passes around the horse's breast and is attached to the saddle. Standard length is 32 inches. Some breast-collars have a neck piece and side straps both of which are adjustable. When used with a saddle it is more properly termed *martingale*.

BREECHING. A wide strap which passes around a horse's rump.

BRIDLE. Head harness consisting of headstall, bit, and reins.

BUCKING-STRAP. A strap placed tightly around a horse's belly to make him buck.

BUCK-STRAP. A leather loop attached to the saddle horn to provide a "hand holt" when riding a bucking horse.

BULL-RIGGING. A broad strap or rope around an animal's body and to which are attached "hand holts" for wild steer riding in rodeos.

BULL-WHIP. A whip with a lash from 15 to 25 feet in length, with a short lead-weighted handle.

BUSCADERO BELT. A broad belt from which two guns can be hung, one on each side.

BUTTON. Woven leather or rawhide knot on quirts, bridle reins, headstalls, and other gear.

CABESTRO *(cah-bes'tro)*. Horsehair tie-rope.

CANTINAS. Saddle-pockets which slip over the saddle horn.

CANTLE. Up-curved back of a saddle.

CATCH-ROPE. Working rope or lariat.

CHAPS. Leather leggings with wide flaps for the protection of a horseman's legs. From the Mexican *Chaparejos*.

CINCH. A wide strap which goes around a horse's belly to hold the saddle on his back. Called *cincha* in some parts.

CONCHA. Silver or metal ornament used on belts, bits, headstalls, and saddles. Saddle conchas are usually termed "string conchas" and come in sets of eight.

CORONA. A fancy saddle pad.

CUFF. Leather gauntlet for guarding the wrists and protecting the shirt sleeves.

CURB-STRAP. Strap which is attached to the bit and passes behind the horse's chin.

DANGLERS. Pear-shaped ornaments of metal which dangle from spurs.

DROVER'S WHIP. A swivel-handled and shot-loaded whip having a lash from 8 to 12 feet long.

DUFFEL BAG. A roll containing blankets and personal effects.

EAR-HEAD. A simple headstall without noseband, browband, or throatlatch, and with a loop or loops for one or both of the horse's ears.

FIADOR. A safety device or throatlatch used on the hackamore. Sometimes called *"Theodore"*.

FIADOR KNOT. An intricate knot used on the fiador.

FRILL. A tassel on a quirt or other gear.

GIRTH. Same as *cinch*.

HACKAMORE. Type of western headstall or bridle without a bit. It consists of headstall, bosal, mecate, and fiador. Commonly used in breaking horses and teaching them to neck rein.

HEADSTALL. Part of a bridle or hackamore that fits over the horse's head. It consists of cheek-pieces, crownpiece, noseband, browband, and throatlatch.

HOBBLES. Cuffs or loops joined together and fastened around an animal's forelegs.

HOLSTER. Leather sheath for a pistol or revolver.

HONDA. Eye on the working end of a *lariat,* or *reata,* through which the rope passes to form a loop or noose.

HORN. Pommel or knob on the front of a saddle.

HORSEHAIR ROPE. A rope of braided horsehair. Best quality is the "clipped" rope made from a horse's mane. When used on a hackamore, it is called a *mecate,* or "McCarty".

HORSE JEWELRY. Various types of metal ornaments used on headstalls, breast-collars, and saddles.

JINGLE-BOBS. Another term for *danglers.*

LARIAT. A throw-rope or catch-rope. Usually made of fiber.

LASSO. A modern term for *lariat.* However, the word is more properly used as a verb—to *lasso.*

LEVIS. Blue denim overalls, named for the maker, Levi Strauss.

MAGUEY *(mah-ghay'e).* Four-strand rope, handmade by Mexicans from the fibers of the aloe plant.

MARTINGALE. A breast-collar used with a saddle.

MECATE. A twisted horsehair rope used on the hackamore for reins and lead-rope. Sometimes called "McCarty".

NECKERCHIEF. Bandanna or handkerchief worn around a man's neck, knot to the rear.

NECKROPE. A rope that encircles a horse's neck and through which the lariat passes to keep horse head-on to a calf or steer after it has been roped.

PIGGIN' STRINGS. Strings used to tie an animal's feet after he has been roped and thrown.

PONCHO. Blanket or oiled cloth with a hole in the middle for the horseman's head.

QUIRT. A short, loaded whip.

REATA. A rope 40 to 85 feet in length made from braided rawhide. The ⅜-inch diameter *reata* is called "light"; 7/16-inch, "medium"; ½-inch, "heavy"; and the 9/16-inch, "extra heavy". Often misspelled *"riata".*

REINS. Leather or rawhide lines attached to the *bit.* By these the rider guides and manages his horse. There are two types of reins, *open* and *closed.*

RIGGING. *Latigo, cinch,* and *rigging-rings,* or gear securing a saddle on a horse's back.

ROMAL. A long flexible quirt or whip attached to closed reins. It measures about 3 feet with its 1-foot "popper", or lash. Sometimes misspelled *"ramal".*

ROPE. A common term for a *lariat*. The two general types of ropes are the *hard-twist*, made from vegetable fiber, and the *reata*, of braided rawhide.

ROPING-REINS. Closed reins used in roping. The standard length is 6 feet.

ROSETTE. A leather tie ornament used both as a decoration and as fastenings on saddles and headstalls.

SADDLE. A leather seat with a high horn and cantle, fastened to a horse's back to accommodate the rider. With its rigging, consists of a tree, horn, seat, cantle, back jockey, skirt, swell, gullet, front jockey, fender (rosadero), stirrup-leathers, stirrups, cinch rings, latigo, conchas and tie-strings.

SADDLE-BLANKET. A blanket or padding between saddle and horse's back.

SADDLE-POCKETS. Leather bags joined together and hung across saddle behind the cantle.

SCABBARD. Open-mouthed leather sheath for a rifle or carbine.

SKIRT ORNAMENTS. Silver ornaments for decorating saddle-skirts.

SLICKER. A raincoat made of oiled canvas. Sometimes called a "fish".

SPUR-CHAINS. Small chains attached to spurs and passing under the wearer's instep. Two or three chains are used.

SPURS. Metal implements attached to the heels of a rider's boots. They usually have a wheel or *rowel* with blunt-ended points and may be hand-forged, plain, silver-inlaid, or silver-mounted, with straight or curved shanks, of $1/8$-, $1/4$-, or $1/2$-inch metal.

SPUR-STRAPS. Leather straps securing spurs to rider's boots. Usually carved or stamped, some are decorated with silver conchas. Some cowboys wear the buckles inside; others wear them outside.

STAKE-ROPE. A picket-rope, or rope for tieing up a horse.

STRING. A tie-leather used on saddles. Also a term for a rawhide thong.

SURCINGLE. Girth or strap passing around the body of an animal.

TAPS. Leather covering or shields over the front of stirrups. The word is from the Mexican *Tapaderos*.

TIE-STRINGS. Leather thongs or rawhide strings that pass through leather rosettes or metal conchas on saddles. Used to tie on blankets and other articles, as well as to hold parts of the saddle together.

TIE-DOWN BOSAL. A pencil bosal with a loop or ring in place of the heel-knot on other bosals.

WAR BRIDLE. Halter used in leading unruly horses; usually a *lariat-noose* placed in the horse's mouth and over his head.

WEAR-LEATHER. Another term for *boot,* used to protect braid in the eyes of hondas and reins.

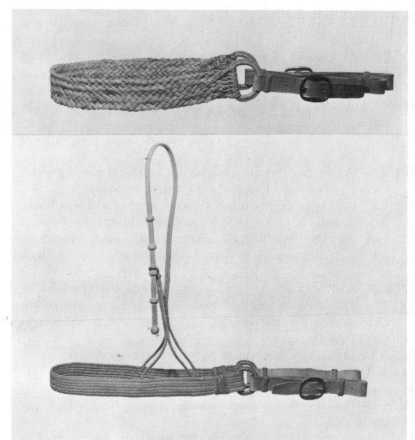

Braided rawhide breast collars made by John Conrad, Bellflower, California.

RAWHIDE BIBLIOGRAPHY

CATALOGUES (Old). Hamley & Company, Victor Marden, Visalia Stock Saddle Company, Walsh-Richardson Company. Pictures of oldtime rawhide braidwork.

COUNTRY HIDES AND SKINS, U.S. Department of Agriculture, Farmers' Bulletin No. 1055, Washington, D.C., revised edition, 1942. Instructions on how to skin an animal.

DOBIE, J. Frank, *The Longhorns*, Boston, 1941. pp. 221-241. Romantic aspects of rawhide.

GRANT, Bruce, *The Cowboy Encyclopedia*, Chicago, 1951. Alphabetically arranged text. Rawhide and Horse Gear.

GRANT, Bruce, *Leather Braiding*, Cambridge, Md., 1950. Leather and rawhide braiding sequences.

GRISWOLD, Lester, *Handicraft*, Colorado Springs, Colo., 1951. How to make rawhide and rawhide handcraft.

HANDBOOK OF AMERICAN INDIANS NORTH OF MEXICO, edited by Frederick Webb Hodge, Bureau of American Ethnology, Bulletin 30, 2 vols., Washington, D.C., 1907-1910. Skin and Skin Dressing, Vol. 2, pp. 592-594.

INDIANS OF THE SOUTHEASTERN UNITED STATES, John R. Swanton, Smithsonian Institution, Bulletin 137, Washington, D.C., 1946. Indian methods of making rawhide. pp. 442-448.

JAEGER, Ellsworth, *Wildwood Wisdom*, New York, 1945. Indian uses of rawhide. pp. 26-27.

LOPEZ OSORNIO, Mario A., *Trenzas Gauchas*, Buenos Aires, 1943. Argentine methods of rawhide braiding.

MASON, Bernard S., *Woodcraft*, New York, 1939. Indian method of making rawhide and uses. pp. 394-422.

RAINE, W. MacLeod, and BARNES, Will C., *Cattle*, Garden City, N.Y., 1930. How cowboys utilized rawhide. pp. 309-313.

RINCON GALLARDO, D. Carlos, *El Charro Mexicano*, Mexico City, 1939. Mexican rawhide horse gear.

SAUBIDET, Tito, *Vocabulario y Refranero Criollo*, Buenos Aires, 1945. Alphabetically arranged text. Gaucho horse gear and the making and uses of rawhide.

HOW TO MAKE A WESTERN SADDLE
by Lee M. Rice

No doubt everyone who has been closely associated with horses has at some time felt a keen desire to build for himself a saddle. Somehow, there is a greater sense of pride in a self-made saddle than in any other part of horse gear.

A visit to a local saddle shop, where one sees the various pieces of equipment, as well as the great array of saddler's tools, displayed neatly on the board back of the saddler's bench, has often dispelled the desire to build a saddle as being too ambitious and expensive. If you have the courage and ambition to start such a project, it is surprising how little equipment and how few tools you can get by with. You must have lots of patience and feel your way carefully. Study each move until you are reasonably sure what you want to do and a lot of your troubles will be eliminated. The one thing that must be built up, before you start such a project, is confidence.

It is true that, for the novice, the making of a saddle will prove one of the most ambitious of all the projects in the making of horse gear. Likewise, it is beset with the most obstacles. But with determination and study, one who has had no previous experience with leather work, can do the job. It would be a great help if the novice saddle maker could have an old saddle around to check with as he progresses with the new job. This would give him a clearer idea of sizes, shapes and dimensions as he follows his instructions. In a saddle shop, one sees stitch horses, draw down stands, as well as machines and other equipment which enable the journeyman to carry out his work with ease and speed. Yet saddles have been made by novice saddle makers with absolutely no fixtures. You simply improvise to fit the needs as various problems arise.

THE DRAWDOWN STAND

The one piece of equipment that is almost indispensable is the drawdown stand. Ninety per cent of the work on a saddle is done on the drawdown stand. It is almost indispensable for the original fitting of the leather to the bare saddle tree. Also, after the leather has been tooled or stamped, one must have some kind of a stand on which to assemble the finished saddle.

Anyone handy with a saw and hammer can easily build a drawdown stand for himself. Little material is required. The cost of the materials, as well as the time and trouble to build it, will be well compensated in the ease and convenience of carrying on the project. At first, the instructions for building a drawdown stand might seem rather complicated. Before proceeding, one should carefully study all detail, as illustrated in *Fig. 1*. It will make the text more simple and more easy to grasp.

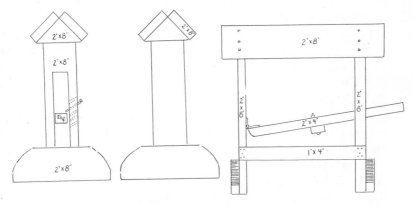

FIG. 1. THE DRAWDOWN STAND

From a piece of 2 x 8-inch planking, cut two pieces about twenty-eight or thirty inches long. With two triangular blocks of the same material, nail these together at an angle of around forty-five degrees. These form the side boards of the stand and should have a slight opening or crack between the bars along the top. This prevents collecting of tacks, nails and shavings. This first step has been very simple.

The next step will be the legs. There are two ways this can be done. One is to use the same material—2 x 8-inch planking. Cut these to any desired length that will make the drawdown stand of convenient height for the user. The back leg will need only to be beveled at the top to fit under the side bars. The front leg of the stand should have a 4-inch strip sawed out of the center, starting at the bottom and extending up about twenty-four inches. The top should be finished the same as the back leg. The purpose of this slot is to accommodate the raising and lowering movement of the drawdown bar. The next step is the foundation to give the drawdown stand needed weight at the bottom to prevent its being too easily overturned. For the foundation, cut two 2 x 8-inch blocks about fifteen inches long. These foundation blocks will then be nailed across the bottom of the legs to rest on the floor for a firm foundation. The top outside corners should be rounded or beveled off. Also, the legs could be cut from 2 x 4″ and set about four inches apart to allow the draw down bar to work freely between them. With these, the foundation blocks should also be used. The next step is the tie brace at the bottom of the stand. At the top of the foundation blocks, nail a 1 x 4-inch strip from the front leg to the back leg to give the drawdown stand rigidity.

The next step will be the drawdown bar. This can be cut from 2″ x 4″ long enough to extend some ten inches through the slot in the front legs to give foot leverage in operating the bar. About six inches above the top of the foundation block, attach the drawdown bar to the back legs with a common heavy gate hinge. Where the drawdown bar works through the slot in the front leg, some means of retaining and releasing the tension on the drawdown strap must be devised. On all drawdown stands used in saddle shops, an iron plate is screwed to the top of the drawdown bar. On one side of the slot is screwed a comb, or strip, of iron with teeth cut in to engage the plate on the drawdown bar. This works on the same principle as the brake on a wagon. But for those with more limited means, a simpler method is to bore a series of holes through the left front leg through which one can slip an iron pin to hold the bar while retaining the tension on the drawdown strap. An iron bolt would serve very well for this purpose. The drawdown bar must be equipped with a cross arm or spreader, the purpose of which is to spread the pull on the drawdown strap. This prevents pulling wrinkles in the seat leather while fitting as well as in putting it down permanently after tooling or stamping. It might be well to state here that one cannot be too careful to avoid pulling wrinkles in the seat leather. Once they are there, they are very hard to smooth out. The cross arm can be cut of 2″ x 4″ about twenty-eight inches long. In the center of the bar, bore a hole through the flat side. With a single bolt, attach this to the drawdown bar just a few inches forward of center between the front and back legs of the drawdown stand. Care should be taken not to draw this bolt too tight. The cross arm should have a free swinging motion forward and backward. Thus, by shifting the saddle forward or backward on the stand, pressure can be put on different parts of the seat. To complete the cross arm, attach a 2-inch buckle at each end, pointing up. Now you will need two

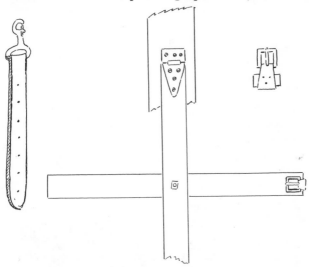

FIG. 2. DETAIL OF DRAWDOWN BAR

leather billets which buckle to each end of the cross arm. For these, cut two strips of leather two inches wide by thirty-six inches long. Get two common harness snaps with a 2-inch slot. Insert the leather strap through the slots of the snaps and double back until both ends of the strap are even. Punch a series of holes for adjustment and buckle to the ends of the cross arm. An adjustment of about twelve inches is necessary as working on different parts of the saddle will require a short or long pull. See *Fig.* 2.

Now, with a couple of pieces of accessory equipment, the drawdown stand will be complete and ready for use. One of these is the drawdown strap. This strap is a strip of leather cut three feet long. It should be about eight inches wide at the center with the ends tapering to about three and a half inches. At each end attach a 3½-inch ring or dee by lapping back about three inches through the ring and fastening with two #8 copper rivets. See *Fig. 3*. Before using, this strap should be thoroughly dampened until pliable and pulled down across a bare saddle tree to give it the proper shape. Next, one will need a spreader bar. This, too, is a very simple piece of equipment. The spreader bar is cut from 1″ x 4″ about twenty-eight inches long, the same length as the cross arm. In each end, saw a V notch about one inch deep and

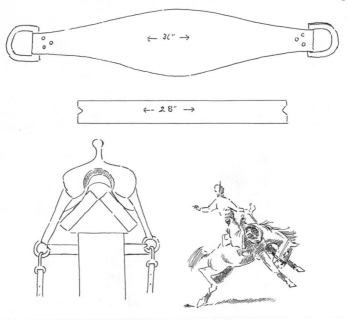

FIG. 3. THE DRAWDOWN STRAP

wide enough to engage the rings of the drawdown strap. The purpose of this bar is to spread the pull on the drawdown strap to prevent pulling wrinkles in the leather as it is being fitted to the saddle tree.

The saddle stand with its accessories is very little equipment compared to that found in a regular saddle shop and the novice saddle maker might think he could dispense even with this.

But the time and effort taken to build one is well spent as he will find that about ninety per cent of the work on a saddle is performed on the drawdown stand. It is a useful piece of equipment and many steps in building a saddle are almost impossible without it.

Tools

The novice saddle maker must have a few tools and he should have these in readiness prior to starting the project. The tool kit of the average journeyman saddle maker contains about two hundred tools. Many are for special purposes which the novice saddle maker will not meet. We consider the following list of about twenty tools a bare minimum for a saddle project. A few could be dispensed with. But the project will be much easier if all tools listed are at hand when the project is started. It must be kept in mind that a few mistakes for lack of a proper tool can prove quite expensive.

In every household there are a few common tools which the novice saddle maker can make use of. A common claw hammer will serve all purposes for the saddle maker. A screwdriver, found in almost every home, will serve all his purposes; also a yard stick and a pair of common pliers. A list of additional tools needed follows:

A pair of cutting nippers for cutting copper rivets and pulling nails and tacks.

One straight knife with a 4½-inch pointed blade.

One round knife.

One #2 common edger and one #10 French edger.

One 10-inch saddler's spike.

Three medium sewing awls and one awl handle.

One #2 drive punch.

One ⅝-inch bag punch.

One #6 drive punch.

One #9 oval drive punch.

One #7 stitch marker or stitch wheel.

One draw gauge, adjustable.

One common compass and one gouge compass for marking stitch lines.

One hand rivet set for use on #8 copper rivet.

One hand brace with one 3/8-inch common wood bit.

One spoke shave and one heel shave.

One pair of flat glazier's pliers.

This list will give the novice saddle maker a good workable tool kit and the use for each individual tool will be fully explained as we get on with the fitting and assembling the finished saddle.

MATERIALS

More materials are needed for a saddle making project than for any of the other projects in the making of horse gear. It is also quite essential that all material be on hand before the project is started. One can keep his interest at a higher pitch if everything required is at hand when needed. All materials can be purchased from one of the many saddlery supply firms. In many localities, there are local saddle shops which sell the necessary supplies for making a saddle. Their prices may be a bit higher but there is the added advantage of much helpful advice.

Before we take up the two main materials—saddle tree and leather—it might be well to list here the accessory materials one will need before starting the project.

One ball of six-cord linen harness thread.

A small piece of harness wax.

Five pounds of cereal saddle paste.

One small can of leather cement.

One box of mixed #8 copper rivets with burs.

One box of 24-ounce tacks.

One box of 12-ounce tacks.

One pound of six-penny wire nails.

One pair 3½-inch saddle dees; one pair 2½-inch saddle dees.

Or one pair 3½-inch saddle rings and one pair 2½-inch saddle dees.

One pair stirrups, any desired width.

Latigos and a set of saddle strings.

One set of string buttons, either leather or metal.

THE SADDLE TREE

The tree is the real foundation of the saddle and much thought should be given to its selection.

The general appearance of the finished saddle depends solely on the type of tree chosen. Therefore, it is essential that much careful consideration be given to the style of tree he selects. These are the main points to consider in selecting a tree: Most important is the length of the seat. Seat measurements of saddle trees range from twelve to eighteen inches, graduating in half inches. A person weighing from 150 to 180 pounds would require a 15-inch tree. It is important not to get the tree too short. A saddle with a tree too short leads to a lot of discomfort in riding. Your next consideration will be height of cantle and width of fork. It must be remembered that one gains about an inch in all measurements over the bare tree when the saddle is finished. Thus, a 2-inch cantle will finish about three inches and a 12-inch fork will finish about thirteen inches. Remember when ordering a saddle tree that all measurements given will apply to the bare tree. Some thought must be given to the height and width of the horn. Again, it must be remembered that the horn will finish out about an inch over the bare tree.

LEATHER

It will require two sides of skirting leather to build a saddle. Skirting comes in three grades: light, medium and heavy. The novice saddle maker will find that the medium grade will be the easiest to work and it makes up into the best all-around saddle. The light weight is used for exceptionally light weight saddles while the heavy weight leather is used only for the most rugged, heavy duty work saddles.

There are two types of skirting leather: eastern and western. The eastern skirting is hemlock tanned and the western skirting is oak tanned. The eastern hemlock tan is the easier of the two to work, while the western oak tan makes a more durable job. The hemlock tan is slightly darker in color than the oak tan and, as the saddle ages, does not take on the cherry red color of the oak tan. For those who live in Canada, the Canadian skirting leather is tanned with fir bark. This Canadian fir tan is not only very beautiful in color but is of a high quality, easy to work and makes up into a very satisfactory job.

There are two ways in which the novice saddle maker may purchase the leather for his project. He can purchase the two necessary sides of skirting from a saddlery supply house. Many saddlery supply firms will sell the leather rough cut, that is, each individual piece is cut roughly to size and shape ready to fit to the tree. Allowances are made for the necessary trimming to the actual fit. This greatly simplifies the project; cutting the leather from the full sides will prove one of the novice saddle maker's most difficult problems and one in which there is the greatest likelihood of errors. Also, many local saddle shops will sell the leather rough cut for a saddle project.

PATTERNS

If one decides to purchase his leather in the full sides and do his own cutting, his first task is to cut rough paper patterns for each individual piece of leather. A heavy grade paper should be used so that a stylus or pencil may be run along the edges. Most of these patterns will offer little trouble. They are simply cut about two inches larger than you will want the finished product. As an example, the standard saddle fender is finished eight inches wide by eighteen and one-half inches high. The tip, when doubled back as through a stirrup, should reach about two-thirds the distance of the height of the fender. These must be taken into consideration when cutting the paper patterns. The same procedure and allowances must be followed in cutting patterns for the skirts, riggings and jockeys. The seat pattern is the only one which will give much trouble. Take a piece of heavy paper and fold it so both sides are even. Along the fold, measure off a distance of twenty-eight inches. Then, from the fold, measure down fourteen inches. Round off the corners on one end to conform roughly to the shape of the cantle. When unfolded, the pattern should look something like a large block letter D and measure twenty-eight by twenty-six inches. See *Fig. 4*. This should take care of a 15- or 16-inch tree. Allowances must be made for smaller or larger trees.

CUTTING

Now that the patterns have been worked out, the novice saddle maker is ready to proceed to the next step—the rough cutting of the leather. For this, he must equip himself with some type of cutting board or bench. The cutting bench should be about two feet wide by at least five feet long. Two by seven feet would be even better. The cutting board should be of as soft a wood as possible. Soft pine is best. Soft wood allows the knife to run easier as well as being much easier on one's sharp cutting tools. As with

FIG. 4. PATTERNS

most every other type of job, saddle making falls into a sort of general routine. Each successive step evolves upon the completion of the step preceding it. One of the first steps, after acquiring all

the materials, is to rough cut the leather and, if it can be done for
the entire job at one time, one can cut to a much greater advantage. In this way, you know just how many pieces of leather go
into the saddle and where each piece is to go. By shifting the

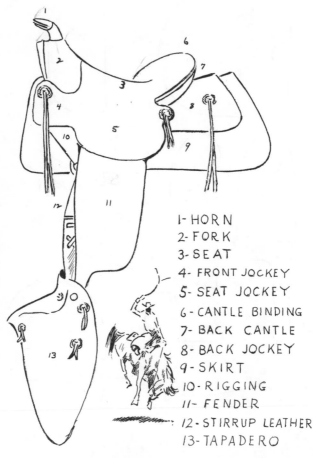

1- HORN
2- FORK
3- SEAT
4- FRONT JOCKEY
5- SEAT JOCKEY
6- CANTLE BINDING
7- BACK CANTLE
8- BACK JOCKEY
9- SKIRT
10- RIGGING
11- FENDER
12- STIRRUP LEATHER
13- TAPADERO

FIG. 5. SADDLE PARTS AND NOMENCLATURE

patterns on the sides of leather, you can better judge the proper
leather for the right part of the saddle. The job always seems to
fall into a better routine of progress when the leather for the
entire saddle is cut at one time. See *Fig. 5.*

The first step in cutting is to square off the back with a straight edge. Then, with the adjustable draw gauge, cut the two stirrup leathers. If you are making a heavy duty saddle, cut these three inches wide. For saddles built only for pleasure riding, two and one-half inches will be wide enough. Unless you have two sides of leather of even weight, it is best to cut both stirrup leathers from the same side to insure even weight and thickness. These stirrup leathers should be cut five and one-half feet long. On the side of leather off which you have just cut the stirrup leathers, cut the seat next. Place the pattern so the front of the seat will be to the top or back of the side of leather. It is very important to get the heavy leather in the front of the seat, letting the back of the seat, which may be lighter in weight, run down toward the belly of the skin. Care should be taken to get the seat out as near one end of the hide as possible without getting into the hard leather of the neck shanks. Also, by keeping the front of the seat to the top of the hide, you are cutting across the side, which insures more even weight to the seat jockeys. Now, from the rest of this side, can come the back jockeys, fork cover, front riggings, and the cantle back.

From the second side, cut the fenders first, keeping the long way of the fender parallel with the top or edge of the side. It must be kept in mind that where two pieces of leather are cut for a right and left side, the pattern must be turned over to prevent cutting both pieces for the same side. Next, get out the two skirts. Be sure the heaviest part of the leather is at the bottom of the skirts. If the skirts should happen to run a little light in weight, they can always be lined without disadvantage. Here, again, keep in mind that the pattern must be turned to get a right and left skirt. If you have cut carefully, you will find you still have enough firm leather to get out the back riggings and other incidentals, such as cantle filler, cantle binding and horn cover. Then, the leather for the ground seat and for covering the stirrups comes from the remainder. If you wish a long pair of tapaderos as well as a flat plate rigging, it may be necessary to get a third side of skirting leather. It is less expensive as well as far less trouble if the leather is purchased rough cut from some saddle supply firm or local saddle shop.

GROUND WORK

The first work on the saddle tree and the real beginning of the saddle follow the rough cutting of the leather. The first piece of leather to go on the tree is the gullet. This should be cut about twelve inches wide where it turns over the rim of the fork, and on somewhat of a circle. At the back of the gullet, it can taper down to about eight inches. On the sides, it should come down to the junction of the fork with the tree bars. Some forks being higher than others, it is always well to check the measurements of the fork before cutting the leather for the gullet. This should be cut of fairly soft leather, as you must make it fit two curves, one opposing the other. The front and sides must be skived to a very thin edge, so that they will blend out smoothly under the leathers that are to cover them. Dampen the leather until it is very pliable so it can be molded to fit its two opposing curves. This can be molded with the hands until it just about fits its position. Next, smear a thin layer of saddle paste on the rawhide of the tree. Place the gullet back in position with about an inch turned over the rim of the fork. Set a tack on each side of the front just above the tree bar. Also, set a tack on top of the fork just in front of the horn. With a pair of pliers, pull the gullet up around the back of the fork. To make it easier to turn the leather around to curve at the back of the fork, the leather can be split at a couple of places to a point almost even with the fork. See *Fig. 6*. Be sure to smooth out any wrinkles which might be pulled into the leather. This can be done easily with the thumb. You will find some slack in the front. With a pair of pliers, pull the leather tight over the rim of the fork. Start the pull low on each side, gradually working to the center under the horn. Tack this edge as you stretch it. The back then should be tacked just under the curve and trimmed flush with the back of the fork. That completes the gullet, unless one wishes to tool or stamp it. This can be done in two ways: The gullet may be tooled before it is put in. With this method, that portion of the leather which is to be tooled must be kept dry, dampening only the leather around the stamping. For the inexperienced, this makes the job more difficult. The second method is to allow the leather and the paste under it to become thoroughly dry, then dampen the outer surface of the leather to permit the tooling. The reason for making the gullet the first operation of the saddle is due to the ground work or ground seat coming next. The gullet would be much more difficult to put in after the ground seat is in place.

There are two types of ground seats which may be put in a saddle. On the Pacific coast, many old-time custom saddle makers use an all-leather ground seat. This type is difficult to put in, but if the job is done right, gives most excellent results. Its greatest advantage is that is affords greater possibilities for shaping a good seat. We will give the details of both methods. The novice saddle maker may decide which method to choose.

ALL-LEATHER GROUND SEAT

For putting in ground seats, all leather should be very wet and pliable at all times. To put in an all-leather ground seat, three pieces of leather are required. The best leather to use for this purpose is that of the neck as it must be quite heavy. The first piece is cut just the shape of the opening or slot in the seat between the tree bars. Allow about a 2-inch margin all around to lap over on the bars of the tree. At the front, this margin can gradually be increased to about three inches to accommodate the anchor nails. Skive this piece to a very thin edge all around except across the front end. The second piece is triangular in shape and fits just back of the fork to give added height and strength. Across the front, this triangular piece can be about the same width as the fork. The sides slope to a point in the center of the seat just back of the stirrup leather slots. This piece can be skived to a very thin edge on all three sides. The third and last piece is cut much the same as a finished seat. In front, it follows the shape of the fork, while the back is shaped the same as the cantle. The sides are cut to extend down to the bottom of the tree bars. This top piece is skived to a very thin edge on across the front and back. The sides must be left to full thickness. See *Fig. 6*. In putting in an all-leather ground seat, it is essential to keep the leather centered on the tree as near as possible at all times.

Now that the seat leather has been cut to the proper shape, the next task is to anchor in the seat. To start the first piece, anchor it at the top of the slot or opening of the cantle with a 24-oz. tack. Now follow around the edge of the leather, setting about two tacks on each side down to the point where the cantle breaks off the tree bars. Be sure to set these tacks on a slant to draw the leather tight across the slot. The next step is to anchor the front. Punch a hole in each of the front corners. Anchor it at the center at the

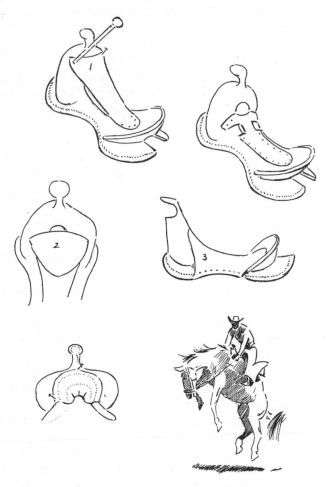

FIG. 6. THE ALL-LEATHER GROUND SEAT

base of the horn. Now, with the spike, stretch the leather forward and outward. After pulling the first corner, release the front center anchor so that all slack can be stretched out of the front while pulling the second corner. The leather should not be stretched too high off the tree bar. For the sidewise or outward pull, give it all the leather will stand. The final step on this first piece is setting the front anchor nails. For these, use a couple of ten-penny wire nails. Set the compass at a point at the center of the fork at the base of the horn. Measure an equal distance on the front corners to locate the point to set the anchor nails. Set these to slant outward to give a slight draw as the anchor nails are seated. Next, with a few box nails slightly larger than a shingle nail, start at the base of the cantle to draw the leather down to the bars. Set the nails to draw slightly outward, at intervals of about one and one-half inches apart. The purpose of this is to pull the leather down on the tree bar. But be sure not to extend this anchoring beyond the slots for the stirrup leathers.

Next, the second or triangular piece of leather is laid just back of the fork. Use saddle paste to hold this piece to the first piece already anchored down. The third, or last piece, is now placed over the first two, after being sure it is centered on the tree. Along each side should be punched a series of four or five holes. Keep these holes, as near as possible, exactly opposite each other. Now, set a nail near the hole at the center of the leather on one side at the bottom of the bar. Through the opposite hole in the other bar, set the spike with a bite, pull the leather down tight and nail. Now come back across to the opposite hole near the nail, release nail and set the spike with a slight bite and pull down as before. You will now have the top leather anchored down tight at the center. Now proceed at each hole, working on alternate sides, to the cantle. Then the same process forward to the fork. Keep all wrinkles out of the seat at all times while this drawing down process is going on. The ground seat is now finished, except cutting the hand hole back of the fork. For this, set the compass at point of center back of the fork at the base of the horn. Scribe a half circle that will make a hole just large enough to slip the open hand down through. It is best to let the ground seat dry a couple of days before cutting this hand hole. For the experienced saddle maker, this is, of course, a rather simple job, for he knows exactly what to do and how to do it. But in trying to describe it to a person without saddle making experience, it sounds more complicated than it really is.

Metal Ground Seat

What is termed, in the saddle trade, as a metal ground seat is much easier to put in. And, for that reason, it is much more universally used throughout the saddle trade. It is used just about everywhere except a few spots in California where the all-leather ground seat is used. If properly put in, the metal seat is as good as can be had. But if improperly put in, it can make the most atrocious seat a rider ever tried to sit in.

The first step in putting in the metal seat is, of course, cutting the metal. For this purpose, get a piece of heavy-gauge galvanized iron. Cut in shape to fit over the opening or slot in the seat of the tree. Leave a margin of about one-half inch. Where this metal comes over the stirrup leather slots, cut out a piece high enough for the stirrup leathers to turn over the top of the bar. Extend the front part of the metal well down along the side of the fork just in front of the stirrup leather slots. Now, drill a series of holes all the way around the back of the metal from stirrup slot to stirrup slot. These holes should be of a size to accommodate a small nail or screw. On the two front prongs, drill two holes in each for a couple of larger nails. Now cut a piece of leather just larger than your piece of metal. Skive the edges thin all around. Dampen this until pliable. Place this leather on the tree under the metal. After getting everything carefully centered in place, proceed to nail or screw the metal down permanently. Sometimes, this metal piece is put in in two pieces to give more flexibility. In this method, the first, or back piece is cut exactly the same but does not extend beyond the stirrup leather slots. The front also is cut very much the same except that the back end is cut a couple of inches longer to extend back over the first piece for support. To put in, anchor the back piece in place first. Then anchor the front piece along the back of the fork and allow the free end to lap back over the first piece a couple of inches for support. This method is just as strong and a bit more flexible. Next, use a triangular piece of leather very much the same shape and size as described before. This is to be used in the same place and for the same purpose as in the all-leather ground seat. As before, this piece should be skived very thin on all three sides. The third piece is cut exactly as previously described. After the front and back have been skived very thin, it is put down as in the all-leather method. Pull down at the sides with a spike until the seat is very tight and firm. Anchor the sides well and let dry. For the novice saddle maker, we suggest that he stick to the metal ground seat. It will give him far less trouble and, if properly put in, is an excellent seat.

Both methods of ground seats can be built as high or low in front as desired by anchoring higher or lower on the fork. And it must be remembered that with both systems all leather must be kept very wet and pliable while putting in the ground seats.

FITTING

The next piece of leather to be fitted to the bare tree is the cantle back. This is a very simple process and may well serve to get the novice saddle maker's hand in the actual feel of the job before meeting more serious problems. First, the leather for the back cantle has been cut almost the actual shape of the back cantle except for being a few inches larger. As with all leather to be fitted, this piece must be dampened until very pliable. The first procedure is to center the leather on the cantle, then, with the hands, draw down tight at the corners. This stretches the leather somewhat into shape. At the top of the tree bars, make a straight cut at each bar, about two inches long. Now pull this center tab of leather down under the cantle and set a tack. Now pull down each corner and make a crease along the bar at the base of the cantle with the rub stick. This gives the shape to the botton of the leather. With a pencil or stylus, mark around the top rim of the cantle on the inside. This gives the proper shape to the top of your back cantle leather. If the saddle is to have a Cheyenne roll, mark off two inches above this mark with the compass. Cut on this line and skive the outer edge as thin as possible. If the saddle is not to have a Cheyenne roll, then leave a one-inch margin and do not skive. That completes the cantle fitting. If the cantle is to have the Cheyenne roll and under two and one-half inches high, it will not be necessary to stamp or tool it as it will not show. If higher than two and one-half inches, or if it is to have a regular binding, it should be stamped or tooled, unless the saddle is to be a plain job.

The next piece to be fitted will be the fork cover. This can be very simple or it may prove difficult, depending on the type of fork. Forks can be had almost any width, from eight inches to fifteen inches. The narrower the fork, the simpler the job of fitting the leather to it. There are two types of swell forks. Those with a high swell, with a lot of under cut and those with a low swell, with no under cut. Before the fork cover can be fitted, it will be necessary to either cover the horn or at least put on the neck wrap. So it might be just as well to dispose of that problem of horn covering.

HORN COVERING

There are two ways to cover a horn. You may like a braided rawhide horn. This makes a nice looking and very serviceable job. It is easy to put on, but also very tricky unless you follow the right system. First, you cut a strip of untanned rawhide, two inches wide by twelve to fifteen inches long, depending on the height of the horn. It must be made clear here that a Mexican or pelican type horn cannot be successfully covered with rawhide. It can only be used to cover the regular type roping horn. After the strip of rawhide is cut, soak it in water until very soft. Wrap this in a towel for a couple of days until it becomes semi-dry but still soft and pliable. Now, place the center of the strip at the center of the horn in front. Lap half the strip over the top of the horn, fold the other half underneath the head of the horn. Stretch this strip around the horn until they meet or cross at the back of the horn. At this point, put a mark on each end of the rawhide strip. Remove the strip and, from this mark to the end, split each end into four strings.

Now you are ready to start the braiding, but remember, it cannot be braided as one would braid a rope. Actually, you have to weave the rawhide around the horn, and this is a very simple process. Center the rawhide back on the horn until the strings start even at the back of the horn. Now, keep all four strings on one side, wrap them around the neck of the horn and set a tack in each string at the bottom. Start with the four strings on the other side and weave them in the opposite direction around the neck of the horn. Weave the string over one and under one. The next string then would go under one and over one. About half-way through this weaving process, it will be necessary to loosen the tacks holding the strings at the bottom so they can be shifted in the weaving process.

After the braiding has been completed, wrap the head of the horn with something soft. A strip of cloth or soft leather will do, or, better yet, a strip of an old rubber innertube. While drying, this will pull the rawhide down firm to the head of the horn. Just before the rawhide is hard, compass a line in about one half inch from the rim of the horn. With an edger, trim on this line. Any surplus rawhide underneath the horn can be trimmed off, also. Next, skive off the ends of all the strings just so the fork cover will cover them. When the horn is thoroughly dry, give the whole job a good coat of shellac.

To cover the horn with leather, which will have to be done with Mexican type horns, there are two methods. First there is the two-piece process. That is, the top of the horn is covered with the same piece of leather which is used for the neck wrap. For this you will need a strip of leather about fifteen inches long. The width will vary according to the size of the horn. You have to figure the size of the horn plus the width necessary to cover the neck. Be sure the neck wrap comes well down under the hole in the fork cover. We will assume the horn has a 3-inch head. In the center of your horn cover, but near one side, compass a circle full three inches. Leave an inch margin around this circle and, of course, on one side, enough leather to make the neck wrap. Set the compass at one and one-quarter inch and set with one point on each side of the circle on the side next to the neck wrap. Punch a hole on the circle at these two points, using a #2 punch. Cut down and out from these holes on a ½-inch circle, then cut on a long upward and outward circle to the end of the strip. Form a point midway between the two points on the circle and measure down until you are sure you have a distance sufficient to cover the neck. Cut the bottom of the neck wrap on a curve, then follow the contour of the top of the wing to the end of the strip. This will give you a wing on each side which will wrap around the neck of the horn. See *Fig. 7*.

This same system can be followed in cutting the neck wrap for a three-piece covered horn. With this method, the horn is covered first, then trimmed and polished. The neck wrap is then put on and when dry, trimmed on a curve on top of the horn. This can be held down with a small screw set near the edge at the center of the curve.

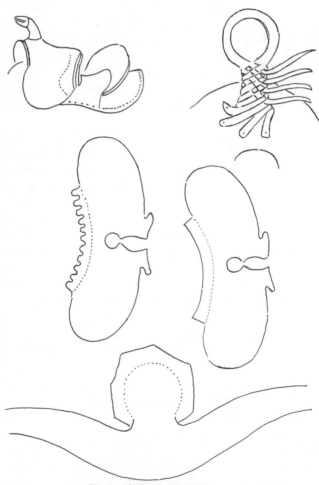

FIG. 7. COVERING THE HORN

To cover the horn, cut a piece of leather roughly the same shape as the under side of the horn. When pulled up tight around the horn, there should be about an inch margin all around the rim of the horn. At the bottom, cut a V notch sufficient to allow the leather to reach around the neck. This notch, as well as the back, should be skived to a very thin edge. Soak this piece until very pliable. Keep the top cover of the horn dry, except the wings of the neck wrap which should be very wet and pliable. Skive all edges of the wings to a very thin edge. With a rasp, roughen the horn to cut the varnish so the cement will adhere to it. You should have a leather cement which will adhere to both wet and dry leather. With a piece of glass, roughen the under, or flesh, side of the top and bottom cover. Coat both pieces, as well as the horn, with cement. Center the top piece on the horn. Pull the bottom piece up snug under the horn. Be sure the back reaches around back of the horn. With a glazier's pliers, crimp the two pieces together around the rim of the horn. With a thin rub stick, work the under part of the horn up snug. Put a slight crease on top around the rim of the horn. Mark off for the stitches with a #7 stitch wheel. After the horn has been stitched, bring the right wing of the wrap around the front of the neck, pull down tight over the back of the fork and tack. Take the left wing around over the first wing in the opposite direction. You will now need a choke strap which is cut from latigo leather about one and one-half inches wide by four feet long. Lap back one end and sew a loop large enough to insert a hammer handle. Wrap this choke strap around the horn, insert the hammer handle for leverage and twist in the same direction as the top wing of the horn wrap. When tight, set a tack in this wing. After the horn is dry, trim around the rim, leaving a margin of one-eighth inch. True up with the spoke shave and edge. Rub and polish the edge and the horn is covered. This same procedure can be followed in covering a three-piece horn.

FITTING THE FORK COVER

Now that the horn has been covered, we will proceed with fitting the fork cover. It must be remembered that all leather must be wet and very pliable for fitting. This applies to all parts of the saddle. Now double the leather back to find the exact center. With a pencil or stylus, draw a line across the leather. After making sure that you have enough leather in front, cut a

2-inch round hole to fit around the horn. If the fork cover is not to be laced down back of the fork, this hole must be large enough to slip over the horn. With exceptionally large horns, it is best to lace the cover back of the fork. Assuming this is to be done, the next move is to cut from the hole out to the edge of the leather. Be sure to cut on the line on which the hole is centered. The heavy part of the leather should always be to the front. Set the leather in place around the horn and fold each end down over the front rim of the fork. Set a tack in front of the fork just above the tree bar at the gullet. With a pencil or stylus, mark around the front rim of the fork. Be sure to press the leather down firm to the fork as you mark. Remove the leather and compass the second mark out one-eighth of an inch from the original mark. This second mark is to serve as the folding line. Now compass out from the fold line, the third line. Cut on this line and skive the edge thin. Now fold this back under the fork cover, being sure to turn it on the fold line. Put the cover back on the fork, being sure to work the turn of the fold down as much as possible. Set the original tacks back in the same spots as before. The fork cover should now appear just as it will in the finished product. If a larger roll is desired, a filler can be put under the roll. These rolls must be cemented in place and, if desired, can be stitched on a line compassed off five-eighths of an inch from the outer edge of the roll. Many saddle markers turn the front of the fork cover over the rim of the fork and tack it just under the rim. Compass a line about one inch out from the fold line. Along this line, pink with a half-inch pinking iron. Be sure to punch a hole with a #6 punch between each cut with the pinking iron. The purpose of these holes is to take up the slack which will accumulate in turning the leather under the rim of the fork.

We now turn our attention to the back. First, work the leather back around the fork, getting as much slack as possible up back of the fork. At the edge of the hole cut for the hand in the ground seat, about one inch out from the fork, cut a notch which will fold over the ground seat. From this notch, cut the leather straight down to the bottom. Then, trim the fork cover to conform with the bottom of the tree bar. Next, fold the leather over the ground seat, then pull forward until tight against the back of the fork and up under the gullet. Keep the circle in the leather level around the horn and if the leather has been kept centered, the split in the cover will be exactly centered at the base of the horn. With a stylus or the back of a knife, start at this point making a mark straight down the back of the fork, allowing the stylus to follow through under the gullet.

Remove the fork cover and when spread out on the cutting board, you will find that this mark runs on a curve. With the round knife, start at the top, cutting on this line until it runs out to the edge of the split. This completes the fitting of one side. Now fold the fork cover over, being sure that both sides of the opening for the horn match. Then mark and cut the opposite side from the one you have just fitted. It is the custom of journeymen saddle makers to always work or fit from the left side.

With certain types of swell forks which have a high swell, as is the case of the Ellensburg or many of the form-fit trees, it will be necessary to lace the fork to take out surplus leather. If the fork is to be laced down over the center of the swell on each side, this surplus leather is taken out after the cover has been fitted as described. Work all slack out of the leather from both front and back, to a point directly under the center of the swell. Mold it with hands until it fits the shape of the fork as nearly as possible. Cut off surplus leather until it can be pinched together with a pair of pliers. This will form a line following the contour of the fork. When the cover is removed and spread flat on the bench, you will have two lines starting at one point on top of the fork. Cut on these lines to the bottom of the fork cover. When these edges are then brought together and laced, the cover will fit the fork. These can also be sewn together with a welt.

FITTING THE SKIRT

The skirt is next on the fitting schedule. This is one exception where the leather should not be too wet. The skirt has been cut by the pattern roughly to shape. With the tree on the drawndown stand, slip the skirt in place under the tree board. Extend the skirt at least two inches from the bar in front, and seven inches in back. Keep the skirt as high up against the ground seat as possible. Set a tack in front under the fork to hold the skirt in place, and one in back in the center of the bottom of the bar.

With the tree now on the bench, pound along the top of the tree bar. This will give you an impression of the top contour of the bar. Take the skirt off and cut along this line. This gives you the shape of the top of the skirt. Now, using the same tack holes, tack the skirt back on the tree. By pressing the skirt up tight against the tree bar, with a pencil or stylus, mark around the tree bar both front and back. This helps to line up the skirts when ready to go back on the saddle. It also leaves a margin for tooling or stamping.

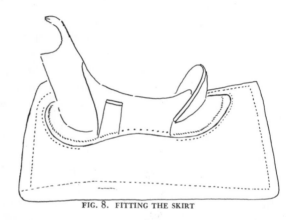

FIG. 8. FITTING THE SKIRT

We will assume now that the skirts are to be square. Next, lay a yardstick along the top of the bar back of the cantle. Be sure to follow the line of the bar. Mark a line one and one-quarter inch from the bar. See *Fig. 8.* Set a mark six and one-half inches from the back of the cantle. This gives you the length of the skirt behind. Set the yardstick on the mark down to the bottom of the skirt. This will give you the back line of the skirt. Be sure to set it back a little at the bottom. This gives a slight kickback to the back line of the skirt. Give as much kickback to the skirt as you like. That takes care of the back of the skirt.

In front, set the compass at one and three-quarter inches and start at the front of the fork and mark around the tree bar to a point at front center. Set the yardstick at this point and mark a line to the bottom of the skirt, slightly forward of vertical. That takes care of the front line of the skirt. Now, at the points where

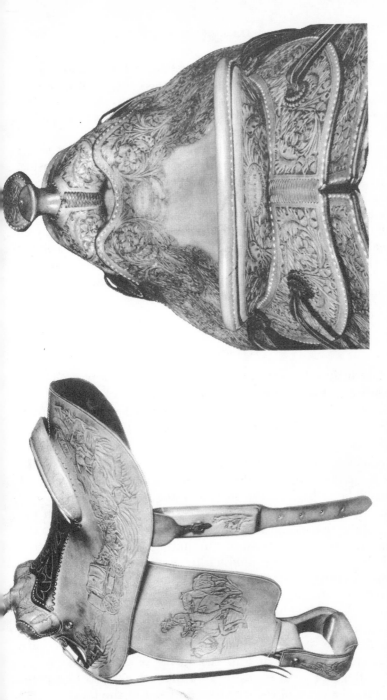

Mother Hubbard type saddle designed by Walt Goldsmith and made by Darrel Ramsdel.

Showing cut of front seat, cut of back fork cover and horn cover.

these lines meet the bottom of the skirt, lay the yardstick level across the bottom. At a point directly under the stirrup slots, set a mark. One-half inch directly above, set a mark. With the yard-stick make a line from this mark to a point where the original line meets the back line of the skirt. Do the same in front. This will give a slight upswing to the bottom of the skirt at a point under the stirrup slots. These instructions might seem a bit confusing, but are very simple when studied. They give more classy lines to the cut of the skirts.

For a round skirt, simply follow the instructions for cutting the top of the skirt. The shape of the bottom can be cut to any pattern the maker desires. Now that you have one skirt fitted, lay it on the other skirt, top side down, and mark around. For transferring the marks around the tree bar have both skirts damp and pound slightly over the marks with a hammer.

FITTING THE SEAT

Before fitting the seat, put one skirt back on the tree. This is necessary to get the proper line to the front seat jockey. Now, take the damp and pliable seat and fold it over and mark the center. Draw a line down the center from front to back. Be sure to keep this line on the under, or flesh, side of the seat. On the top of the cantle, make a mark exactly in the center of the cantle. Also make a mark in the center of the ground seat at the back edge of the hand hole, back of the fork. Put the seat on the tree, line up the mark down the center of the seat with the mark in the center of the cantle, and set a tack. See Fig. 9. Be sure to keep the tack a little back of the rim of the cantle to insure covering the tack holes with the cantle binding. In front, line the seat up with the mark in the ground seat at the hand hole. Set a tack in the fork to insure keeping the seat centered on the tree. It might be well to mention a few things to keep in mind. The seat is the most difficult part of the saddle to fit. Proceed slowly and study out each move. Keep the seat centered on the tree. If the saddle is to have a Cheyenne roll, leave at least two inches of the seat extending back of the cantle. In front, be sure the seat extends to a point even with the front of the tree bars, in front of the fork.

Now that the seat has been centered on the tree, press down firmly all around the rim of the cantle with the hands. At a point one inch up from the junction of the cantle with the tree bar,

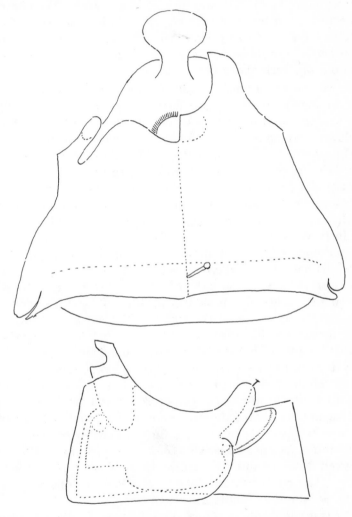

FIG. 9. FITTING THE SEAT

punch an awl through the seat from the bottom. Set the awl about three-eighths of an inch away from the cantle. Compass a one and one-quarter inch circle under this awl mark on the top side of the seat. Keep the awl mark at top center of the circle. This circle will give you the ear for the back button of the seat. Follow the same procedure on the opposite side. At a point one-half inch just back of these buttons, slit the seat out to the bottom. Do not cut sraight down, but backward far enough to allow the back of the seat jockey to extend to a point even with the back of the button. Now press the seat down firmly to the cantle all around and set a tack about one inch above the ear to keep them in place.

Now we give our attention to fitting the front of the seat. From the front edge of the seat, split down the center line to a point about two inches from the back edge of the hand hole. Put the drawdown strap on and draw the seat firmly down to the ground seat. Be sure to keep the seat centered and don't worry too much about wrinkles as the seat is wet and they can be taken out later. With the seat pulled down firm, set the compass in the center of the fork under the base of the horn. Compass a line to conform with the curve of the hand hole, keeping it out about five-eighths of an inch. We will assume you are fitting the left side of the seat. With a French edger, start at the top of this line just compassed around the hand hole and cut on this line down to the center line on the seat. Do not cut more than half of this circle. This cut will give you a starting point as well as allowing the seat leather to fit down more snugly around the fork. At the left top of this cut, decide how high you want the seat to extend up on the fork. From this point, with a pencil or stylus, mark the shape you like to the front of the seat. In case of a swell fork, cut under to the junction of the fork with the tree bar. This is the most tricky cut of all to fit. It must be remembered that you are fitting to the bare tree and must make allowances for the fork cover and rigging. You must exercise care or you will find this cut is too tight when you assemble the finished saddle. Slick forks give no trouble, but with swell forks, be sure to keep the front of the seat well up on the fork. The cut under the fork must allow for fork cover and rigging. See photo of saddle seat, *Page* 169

With this cut made, it allows the leather to be pulled around snugly under the fork. With the awl, set a mark on the tree bar where the front strings are to come through. Stick the awl through the seat leather to match this mark. Set the compass on this point and mark a two and one-quarter inch circle. This will be the front seat button. Tack the seat leather to the tree bar at this point.

With the French edger, trim off all surplus leather to just within the front edge of the skirt. With the compass, mark a line in five-eighths of an inch from the front edge of the skirt. This will give you the front line of the seat jockey. Now, from the back of the button circle, mark around to the cut just under the fork. The side seat jockey can be cut any shape to suit the maker. However, there are three points here it is well to remember. Start the front of the jockey at a point directly under the center of the fork. The back end should extend to a point even with the rear of the back jockey button. The bottom of the jockey should not reach below the skirts. To cut the bottom of the front seat jockey, measure down from three to three and one-half inches from the cut under the fork to a point on the front end of the seat jockey. From this point, run the compass along the bottom edge of the skirt to the front end of the seat jockey. This will give you your bottom line of the seat jockey.

This completes the laying out of the seat. Remove the seat and cut on the lines you have marked out. Before removing the seat, mark a line around the top rim of the cantle with a soft pencil. Start at the bottom on each side and work toward the top center of the cantle. It will be necessary to remove the three tacks holding the back of the seat. But remove one at a time as you mark. This prevents the seat from slipping out of position. With one side of the seat cut out, fold it over and mark the opposite side. Match up the mark around the rim of the cantle. This should bring the two ears for the back buttons in line. You might have to shift one a little, which is all right. Next, match up the compassed line around the hand hole to get the front of the seat even. Then stick an awl or set a tack through the center of the front and back buttons. The center line of the seat might show, at this stage, that you have folded a little past center. That is all right, but never fold short. From the tack or awl holes, compass off the front and back buttons. When you get this side cut, you have the most difficult fitting job of the whole saddle finished. Be sure to smooth out all wrinkles on the seat before it dries.

This takes care of all fitting except the riggings and back jockeys. For the novice saddle maker, it is better to leave the fitting of the back jockeys until needed or after the saddle is nearly finished. As will be explained later, this will make the job much easier.

RIGGINGS

Riggings are not difficult to fit and a study of *Fig. 10* should explain them. Riggings have become standardized into three types, full double, three-quarter double, and three-quarter single. Of these types, there are two styles: Ring rigging, and the all-leather flat plate. The latter is much more difficult to fit than the ring rigging. The all-leather flat rigging must be cut from one piece of leather and it must be lined. Therefore, it requires much more material than the ring rigging. *Fig. 10* will give you an idea of the shape in which the top must be cut. The shape of the bottom depends on the position of the plate and whether it is to be single or double. However, the all-leather rigging is suitable for only one position, the three-quarter position and its variations of five eighths and seven-eighths. It must also be lined with the plate between the rigging and its lining. It must be sewn all around the edge as well as the hole above the plate to give it strength. The plates should be set in with four #8 copper rivets. Some plates require six rivets. Keep the burrs of the rivets on the under side of the rigging. On all types of rigging, except full double, be sure to keep the back edge of the front rigging far enough forward to have full clearance of the stirrup slots. This allows full freedom in the forward swing of the stirrup leathers.

With the ring riggings, there are three methods of fastening the leather to the rings. For the full double, use two #8 copper rivets in each front rigging as well as the back dees. These will set high enough so that the rivets will be covered by both the front and back jockeys. With the three-quarter riggings, rivets can be used in a plain or work type saddle. The next, and most universally used method, is the three-hole lace. This is done by punching three holes with a #10 punch in a triangular position, keeping the two lower holes in about three-quarters of an inch from each side. The top hole is midway between the bottom holes and about an inch up. To start the lace, pull a ½-inch leather lace through the two bottom holes until both ends are even. As the laces are pulled through the holes, give each a half twist, bring around over the edge of the rigging and pull back through the bottom holes again. Next, bring both laces through the top or center hole. Take one lace through each of the bottom holes. To anchor, tuck each lace under a lap on the back side. That completes the three-hole lace.

The third method is known as the Spanish or half-diamond lace. After the rigging has been turned back through the ring, set

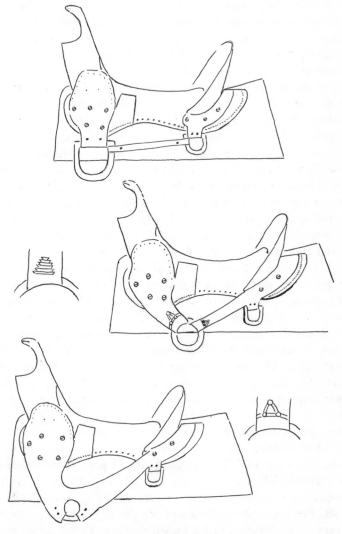

FIG. 10. SADDLE RIGGINGS

a tack through it so it can't give or slip out of position. From a point about one-half inch in from the edge just above the ring, draw a line up and in towards the center of the rigging. Have these lines end about one-half inch apart at the top. These are the guide lines for setting the holes for the lacing. The lace is cut one-half inch wide by about eighteen inches long. These should be of calf-skin or soft leather. For this job, two pieces of equipment will be necessary which were not listed before. These are a stitch horse for holding the work firm and a medium-sized diamond awl. At the bottom of the guide line, set the awl at an angle with the top pointing out or away from the guide line. Pull the lace through from the back side. Carry across the front of the rigging and go back through a hole at the same point on the opposite guide line. For the next lace. start the awl in the same position on the first guide line at a point just above the first cross lace and down on the opposite line. These sloping guide lines will shorten each succeed-ing lace, finishing with a very short one at the top. It should take from seven to nine cross laces to do the job. The awl should be of such size so the ½-inch lace pulls tight through them. When fin-ished, smooth down the lace with a rub stick. With a little prac-tice, this makes a very neat job on a fancy saddle.

With our modern saddle trees, it is no longer practical to put the rigging all the way over the fork. Therefore, more bearing surface must be allowed on the tree bar as well as the fork. Five 1¼-inch #12 flat head wood screws should be used to anchor the front rigging to the tree. Set three screws on the bar and two on the fork. Two 1-inch #12 wood screws on each side will hold the back rigging. The back rigging may go all the way across the back of the cantle but not necessarily. A rigging anchored in this manner will withstand all strains necessary for a heavy working saddle.

As for the positions of the rigging, these have been standardized to the full double and the three-quarters in either single or double. With the full double, the point of pull of the front rings or dees should fall directly under the center of the fork. With the three-quarters, the pull comes directly under a point just back of the fork. For the seven-eighths and the five-eighths, move the three-quarters either forward or backward slightly. These positions have no practical purpose. As for the back dee, it should hang at a point just back of the forward point of the cantle. With all types of rig-ging, the front ring or dee should hang with at least one-third of the ring off the lower edge of the skirt. One-half of the skirts

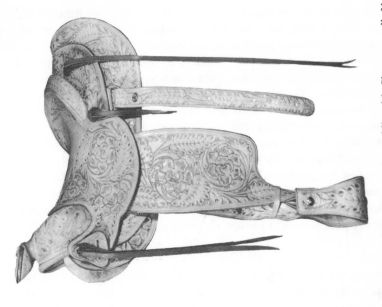

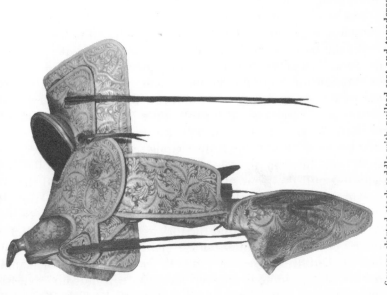

Round skirted low roping saddle with Cheyenne roll. Note line of skirts and jockeys. Made by Lee Rice.

Square skirted stock saddle with quilted seat and tapaderos. Note line of skirts and jockeys. Made by Lee Rice.

should be on the tree while hanging the rigging. Be sure to check accurately the forward and backward position of the rigging. If the vertical position is off a bit, it makes no difference. But if the horizontal position is off much, the saddle may have a tendency to crawl or pull to one side. There are several points on the tree to check from. For the vertical position, the best is a point exactly at the center of the fork at the base of the horn. For the horizontal position, check from the top of the tree bar just where it emerges from under the cantle. These are the safest two spots to check from. Likewise, a point at the exact center of the top of the cantle makes a good checking point. Once the rigging is fitted, edge and polish the edges with a rub cloth. A piece of light canvas makes an excellent rub cloth. Then anchor the front rings to their permanent positions on the tree.

ASSEMBLING THE SADDLE

We now have the horn covered and the rigging anchored in its permanent position. Next, with the spoke shave and heel shave, shape the ground seat. Be careful to keep the seat as smooth as possible by removing all high spots.

The next permanent piece to go on is the fork cover. Dampen the cover until quite pliable. Place it around the horn and lace down the back of the fork. Put a light coat of saddle paste over the fork. Take care that it does not squeeze out around the horn or through the holes for the back lacing. Work the front roll of the fork cover down around the front rim of the fork. Set a six-penny nail at each end of this roll at the junction of the fork with the bars. Set the nail to draw downward and in. At a point on the tree bar, just back of the front rigging, pull the fork cover down snug over the shoulders of the swell with pliers or a spike. This will also pull the front of the cover down snug around the rim. Be sure to keep the hole around the horn level. Next, turn the saddle over and pull the cover snug under the gullet. Be sure to work out all slack behind the fork as you make this pull. Tack the cover under the gullet on a straight line and trim off surplus leather. Rub this edge down smooth with a rub stick or hammer handle. If the saddle has a swell fork, you will now find you have much slack to gather in around the base of the fork. To do this, work all leather forward. Cut a V notch out under the front button. Be sure the button will cover the cut. This will take out a lot of slack. Then keep molding the cover under the fork and tack as the slack is gathered in. As the leather dries, pound out the wrinkles by tapping lightly with a hammer. Be sure to tap on an extra piece of leather to prevent leaving hammer marks on the fork cover.

The next step is the Cheyenne roll and putting on the back cantle. First, cut a strip of fairly heavy leather two and one-half inches wide and long enough to reach around the rim of the cantle. This is the cantle filler and can be cut straight or on a slight curve to fit the rim of the cantle. The curved type is easier to put on but the straight makes the better roll. Skive one side to a very thin edge. Put this on very wet. Start at the center of the filler and tack the thin side to the cantle. Tacking it about one-half inch down from the edge of the cantle. As you work towards each end, keep gathering in enough slack so the filler can be rolled back at a right angle to the cantle. Keep testing as you go along, as it requires more slack as you go over the extreme curve of the cantle. If you find it is too tight, loosen each end and give it more gather. When right, cut off surplus ends at the bottom of the rim. With a rub stick, crease around the rim of the cantle to give it a breaking point. Now coat the back of the cantle with saddle paste and put the back cantle cover in place. Set a tack under the cantle between the bars. Pull each end down tight until the cover is smooth across the back, then tack each end. Now roll the filler back in position. With a hammer handle, rub top of the roll until it is flat and smooth in a position at a right angle to the cantle. Also, keep the back cantle cover worked smooth against the tree as well as up under the roll. Allow this to dry thoroughly before trimming the roll into shape. To trim a Cheyenne roll, compass out two inches from the inside of the cantle rim and round in at the bottom so the button ears will fit under. After this cut, true up with a spoke shave and edge. If a regular binding is desired, follow the same procedure but use a narrower filler and do not roll back.

Next on the routine is the seat. First, be sure that you now have the stirrup slots, for hanging the stirrups, cut in the ground seat. The indentations on the tree indicate where they should be cut. If you have used a metal ground seat, they should be cut while putting in the ground seat. Be sure to put back in the seat all plugs that were cut out and tack lightly so they can be easily removed after the seat has been put in and dried. You will need this support while smoothing out the regular seat. Also, they have to be so they can be easily removed when you are ready to hang the stirrup leathers.

Edge the seat, both top and under side, and polish the edges good with a rub cloth. Well-polished edges add greatly to the finish of a saddle. Dampen thoroughly only that part of the seat which will come in direct contact with the tree. Be sure to keep the side seat jockeys dry. Place the seat on the tree centered so the original mark around the cantle fits into place. See that the cut-out around the hand hole in front is even. Place the drawdown strap across the seat and apply some pressure. Loosen this pressure as often as necessary to work out the wrinkles which will be pulled into the seat. You will find that now you seem to have much surplus into the seat. Keep working this to the center under the drawdown strap. Each time you apply pressure on the strap, rub the top of the strap with a rub stick. Or a smooth beverage bottle will serve this purpose. When the seat is down smooth, punch the two holes in the front jockeys for the front saddle strings. Place a spike in the lower of these holes and at a position where the strings are to come through the tree bar in front. Pull forward and upward to draw the jockey around firm under the swell of the fork. Draw both sides and tack in front.

Now you will find the ears for the back seat buttons stand out away from the cantle. Press the damp leather down firmly against the cantle. From the top of the button ear, cut forward and upward to the cantle. This will allow the ear to lay in snugly under the Cheyenne roll. The lower point of the roll will show where to make this cut. If you find this will make the cut too low, trim off the point of the roll to bring the cut a little higher. Be sure the cuts are about even on both sides. If the saddle is not to have a quilted seat, you now raise the seat and coat the ground seat with saddle paste. Have the paste come to the top rim of the cantle and to the bottom of the tree bars. Coat forward between the stirrup slots but be sure not to get any paste on the plugs in the stirrup slots. As the seat has now been shaped to the tree, it will go back in place without more trouble. Now you will have a 2-inch margin above the cantle rim. Pull this back over the roll and cement it down. Then trim to fit the roll and pop stitch, stitching in about one-half inch from the outer edge of the roll. You are now ready to put on the cantle binding.

If a quilted seat is desired, it must be fitted before the seat is removed for the paste. For the quilted seat, use a soft leather, either calfskin or horsehide. Before fitting, a guide line should be marked out on the seat. Start this line at the top of the ear for the back jockey button, swinging up and forward to the front of the seat. These guide lines should be the same on both sides of the seat. At the narrowest point, just forward of the middle of the seat, there should be at least seven inches between these guide lines. Be careful not to get the quilted seat too narrow. Cut a piece of the quilting leather roughly the shape of the finished seat. Stretch this on the seat, being careful to smooth out all wrinkles. With a soft pencil, mark it on the guide lines. The front edge of the seat will give you the shape of the front. Next mark around the rim of the cantle. Be sure to leave enough material to lap back on the Cheyenne roll. Now remove and spread flat on the bench. With a ⅜-inch pinking iron, pink both sides and the front. You are now ready for the quilting.

An easy method for marking the design on a quilted seat is to make a paper pattern the size of the seat. Fold this in half. On one side, mark the design. With a stitch wheel, mark the design through on the other side. This gives you an all-over design. Lay this on the leather to be quilted. With the stitch wheel, mark the design on the leather. Cut a piece of wool skin slightly smaller than the seat leather. Skive the edges all around to a thin edge. Clip the wool as short as possible, as you cannot quilt through long wool. Cement the woolskin at the edges to the quilting leather. Quilt on a light sewing machine. Cut a piece of sponge rubber to fit and cement to the quilted seat. Center the quilted seat on the main seat by using the guide lines. Set a few tacks in the pinking to hold in place, then stitch through the pinking with an overstitch, using a heavy linen thread. Now fit and stitch the cantle binding and anchor the back rigging which has been left loose for working convenience.

You are now ready to put the skirts on permanently. First, after the woolskins have been pasted on and sewn, trim and edge both the skirt and the woolskin and polish the edges. Lace together at

the back. Be sure lacing will be covered by the back jockeys. Now
center the skirts on the tree, leaving the proper margin both ir
front and back. Tack securely to hold skirts in place while boring
the holes for the saddle strings. Bore through both tree and skirts
Remove the skirt and trim any roughage around the holes. Draw
the saddle strings through the holes, being sure to keep the string:
between the skirt and woolskin. Smooth the holes on the tree, both
top and bottom. Cut the rawhide out between the holes so the
strings can be tapped down flush to the tree. This eliminates an
bumps or high spots where the strings go through the tree. Now
string the skirts back on the tree. This will bring them to the righ
position. Anchor under the fork with about three six-penny nails
Bleed a couple of short strings through the skirts at the edge o
the tree bar. Draw the ends firmly up over the tree bar and tack
This will anchor the skirts firmly to the tree behind.

Now to fit the back jockeys. First, fit the jockey to the contou
of the cantle. At the top, set a mark on the line where the two
skirts come together, just back of the cantle. At the back, set a
mark about three-eighths of an inch away from the point where
the skirts meet at the top. Draw a line between these points and
cut the top of the jockey on this line. You now have the from
and top of the jockey fitted. Turn this over and fit the opposit
jockey. Stitch these together at the top with an overstitch. Plac
the jockeys on the tree and mark the front holes under the bac
buttons of the seat jockeys. Punch these holes about one-eighth o
an inch back of the marks. This extra pull allows you to take ac
vantage of the off-center cut at the top of the jockeys to pull th
outer edge of the jockey down over the edge of the tree bar. Th
jockey will thus lay firm on the skirts. With a spike, pull th
jockeys firm on the tree and tack. This can be done by pulling t
the string holes in the tree. If the jockeys are to be square, mark t
conform with the back and bottom lines of the skirts. Use th
bottom line of the front seat jockey as a measure for depth. Wit
a square-skirted saddle be sure to get a true lineup of skirts an
jockeys. With a round-skirted saddle you must depend mostly o
your eye and good judgment for proper balance between skir
and jockeys.

The fenders are simple to cut. The standard size is eight inches wide by eighteen inches long. This can be cut to a variety of shapes to suit the maker. When folded back, as through a stirrup, the tips should reach about one-third up the height of the fender. These tips can be cut for either a 2½- or a 3-inch stirrup roller. The standard stirrup leather is five and one-half feet long. Round off the heavy end and punch a double row of nine lace holes with a #9 oval punch. The light end can be attached to the tips of the fenders by either sewing or riveting. In this operation, keep flesh

FIG. 11. STIRRUP LEATHERS

side to flesh side. Next, fasten the stirrup leather to the fender at the top. Either rivet or lace with a three-hole lace. Care should be taken to bend the stirrup leather into proper position before fastening at the top. The inside leather must be shorter. Next, with a #9 oval punch, punch a double row of three-lace holes in the end of the fender tip. Set the first two holes back about five-eighths of an inch from the end of the tip. Use the opposite end of the stirrup leather to get proper spacing of these holes. It will be easier to hang the stirrup leathers if the two front strings of the saddle are left unfastened until the stirrup leathers are in place. This completes the saddle except for stirrups. See *Fig. 11.*

STIRRUPS

Stirrups can be plain or leather covered. If plain, wear leather should be placed in the bottom of the tread and around the rollers. There are two methods of leather covering stirrups. For a laced stirrup, use two pieces of leather for each stirrup, one for each side, meeting at the bottom. To cut the leather for lacing, measure around the stirrup with a string at the top, bottom and at the bend of the stirrup. This will give the size and shape of the

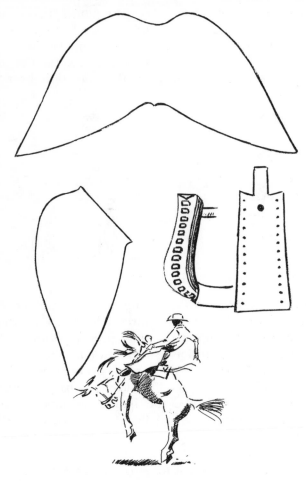

FIG. 12. STIRRUPS

leather for lacing around the stirrup. Leave a tab of leather at the top as wide as the stirrup to fold back over the top of the stirrup and under the lacing. Compass a line down each side, in far enough to prevent the holes from tearing out. Mark off the holes on this line close enough so each lap of the lace will lay snug against the other. At the bottom, trim to fit, and tack. To start, remove the bolt from the stirrup. Place the leather on the inside of the stirrup between the roller and the wood. Put the bolt back through and tighten. Now bring the tab back over the top of the stirrup and tack. Then proceed with the lacing. Finish with wear leather. Leather must be damp and pliable.

The second method is to sew the leather. This requires four pieces of leather for each stirrup. The inside, or liners, should not be too heavy. Have these liners very damp and pliable. Place on the inside of the stirrup, the same as for lacing. The outside leathers should be dry. Coat both inside and outside with leather cement. Pinch these together with a pair of pliers. Keep the outside flush with the stirrup and trim to fit at the bottom. Mark a stitch line around the stirrup and sew from the outside. Finish with wear leathers in the tread. Sew with two needles, the same as in sewing the horn and cantle binding.

The modern tapadero is simple to make as it is cut in one piece. First, take a piece of heavy paper and fold at the center. Using the fold as the top of the nose, mark out the exact shape of tap you want. These are the measurements you will need. The top of the nose should be in nine inches. See *Fig. 12*. From top to tip of wing, the tap can be cut from fourteen to twenty-four inches. The width of the wing at the bottom of the stirrup should be at least ten inches. Cut the leather exactly to the pattern. It might be necessary to cut several patterns before you get one to suit.

To string a tap to the stirrup, first dampen the nose or center of the tap and fold it together. In front, directly under the tip of the nose, fasten the wings together with a string and two buttons. By using the edge of a bench, break the nose in about three inches from the top. Be sure to hold the wings even when doing this. While the nose is damp, it can be worked into proper shape. With the tap in proper shape, fit the stirrup in and mark the two holes for the stirrup bolts. Now bolt the taps to the stirrups. It will be necessary to use a longer bolt than the original stirrup bolt. For this purpose, use a $3/8 \times 5\frac{1}{2}$-inch bolt with a silver or monel covered head. Now get the stirrup in the exact position you want in the tap. With a diamond awl, punch two holes in each wing at the widest part of the stirrup. Pull a string through the inside wing, take it through under the bottom of the stirrup, and through the outside wing. Fasten these strings by bleeding them through over a button, the same as stringing a saddle. Press the top of the nose in firm against the stirrup. With a diamond awl, punch two holes on each side of the front about two and one-half inches down from the top. Punch from the front, but keep these holes wide enough apart so they will be supported by the sides of the stirrups. This position can be marked by punching with a small awl from the inside just inside the stirrups. Put the strings with button through from the front. Take the strings through the stirrup. At the back of the stirrup, punch two more holes in the wing of the tap and bring the strings through and bleed over a button. Be sure to keep this last set of holes low enough so they do not inter fere with the stirrup leather around the stirrup roller. Taps can not be put on over leather covered stirrups. Most saddle makers put a piece of woolskin in the nose of the tap to prevent wear on riding boots. This can be put in with leather cement.

THE STRAP

A rope strap should complete the project. Cut this of soft string leather, three-quarters of an inch wide by thirty inches long. In one end, have a slit long enough to loop over the horn. With five-eighths bag puch, punch a hole through the fork cover about three inches down from the horn on the right side of the fork. This can be done after the cover has been put on the fork and is dry. Raise the leather above this hole with a screwdriver. Tape the opposite end of the rope strap and insert it through the hole far enough to set a 1-inch oval head wood screw in the fork just above the bag punch slot. Be sure to keep the flesh side of the strap up or out.

The saddle should now be oiled with pure neat's foot oil. This will give it a darker, richer color.